THE OFFICIAL BOOK

Jordan Paramor is a freelance writer who has contributed to a wide range of magazines and websites including *Smash Hits, Heat, Empire* and Worldpop.com. She has worked closely with Steps on many occasions and was the author of the bestselling *Steps: The Official Book*.

THE OFFICIAL BOOK
STEPS IN PRIVATE

JORDAN PARAMOR

Virgin

This edition first published in Great Britain in 2001 by
Virgin Publishing Ltd
Thames Wharf Studios
Rainville Road
London
W6 9HA

First published in 2000 by Virgin Publishing Ltd

Copyright © Steps 2000
Text by Jordan Paramor

All photographs © David Venni 2000
Supplied courtesy of Idols Licensing and Publicity Ltd

The right of Jordan Paramor to be identified as the Author of this Work has been asserted by her in accordance with the Copyright, Designs and Patents Act, 1988.

This book is sold subject to the condition that it shall not, by way of trade or otherwise, be lent, resold, hired out or otherwise circulated without the publisher's prior written consent in any form of binding or cover other than that in which it is published and without a similar condition including this condition being imposed on the subsequent purchaser.

A catalogue record for this book is available from the British Library.

ISBN 0 7535 0577 0

Typeset by Phoenix Photosetting, Chatham, Kent
Printed and bound in Great Britain by Mackays of Chatham PLC

Contents

1	Steps: The Saga	1
2	Claire In Private	7
3	The Backstage Secrets	18
4	Lee In Private	41
5	It's Showtime!	51
6	Faye In Private	63
7	Step On It!	73
8	H In Private	81
9	Tragedy! It's Time For Work	91
10	Lisa In Private	98
11	After The Work Is Done ...!	107

1 Steps: The Saga!

By the end of the year 2000 Steps will have played to an incredible 700,000 people as they sing and dance their way around the UK, wowing audiences and winning over more and more fans each and every time they perform. Ever since the first heady days back in 1997, when they were performing in nightclubs and dreaming of stardom, there was no way anyone could ignore the all-smiling, all-Technicolor popsters!

They were brought together through an advert in *The Stage* magazine, but back then little did Claire Richards, Lisa Scott-Lee, Lee Latchford Evans, Ian Watkins (H) and Faye Tozer know that they would change the face of pop and win themselves a place in the record books.

The second they landed on Planet Pop in a flurry of glitter, big smiles and even bigger tunes, they captivated pop fans and left everyone wondering what they were going to do next. And

Steps In Private

what they did next was become the brightest, glitziest, most entertaining band in the pop world. They're an award-winning number one-scoring band and there ain't no stopping them now! So how did they get to this point? Let's have a quick look back at Steps' incredible history . . .

Steps released their first single, "5,6,7,8", in November 1997 and the line-dancing extravaganza immediately grabbed the attention of the nation. The single stayed inside the Top 40 for a whopping three months, sold an incredible 300,000 copies in Britain alone, and left pop peeps begging for more. And they soon got it in the shape of the fun-packed, dancealong hit "Last Thing On My Mind" in April 1998. In August 1998 they released the huge summer tune "One for Sorrow" which had every fashionable finger in the country dancing around in the air. But the public wanted more still, and they were only satisfied when the Steppers released their brilliant debut album *Step One* in September 1998. It went on to become one of the most successful albums of the 90s and went five-times Platinum. There was no stopping them!

Likewise there was no stopping the incredible "Tragedy/Heartbeat" double A-side which was released in November 1998 and spent a stonking sixteen weeks in the Top 40, and reached

Steps: The Saga!

the number one spot after nine weeks in the charts. It created yet another fantastic dance move which had such an impact that to this day "Tragedy" is one of the most played songs at clubs and parties up and down the country. Shortly afterwards the gang joined the likes of Billie, B*Witched and Cleopatra on stage at the BRIT awards where they all performed a stunning Abba medley!

"Better Best Forgotten" certainly wasn't forgotten when it was released in March 1999 and became another enormous hit. The Step One tour kicked off at the same time, instantly captivated audiences up and down Britain and won Steps a whole new breed of fan – parents!

"Love's Got a Hold On My Heart" was released in July and became the summer anthem of 1999, reaching number two in the charts.

That summer Faye, Lisa, Claire, H and Lee jetted off to the USA where they'd been invited to support their pal Britney Spears on tour, and were welcomed with open arms by the fun-loving Americans.

Steps returned to Britain and prepared to release their second album. With the public's appetite already whetted, pop lovers were crying out for another album. So when "After The Love Has Gone" hit the charts in October they

Steps In Private

were close to tears with anticipation. All their dreams came true when *Steptacular* was released two weeks later. Needless to say it flew straight into the number one spot and rocketed Steps even higher up the pop ladder!

What happened next scored Steps a place in the record books, and also won them a prestigious BRIT award. After the Step One tour word had spread about Steps' outstanding live performances, and the band completely sold out a 33-date arena tour – the largest arena tour in British pop history! Christmas 1999 was made all the more sparkly and enjoyable with the release of the double A-side single "Say You'll Be Mine/Better The Devil You Know". Steps also sold more albums in 1999 than any other British artist, notching up 1.82 million sales of *Step One* and *Steptacular*. What a brilliant end to a brilliant year!

While 1999 was without a doubt Steps' year, who could have predicted, that 2000 would be even better? In February the band were honoured for their incredible sell-out tour at the BRIT Awards when they were presented with a special award for Best Selling Live Act. Lee and H had to guard the ever-glamorous Faye, Lisa and Claire closely due to the fact that the girls were wearing over one million pounds worth of diamonds! They truly are pop gems!

Steps: The Saga!

The popped-up club track "Deeper Shade Of Blue" was released in April 2000 and was accompanied by one of the coolest and most talked-about videos of the year. Shortly afterwards they were also presented with the Recording Artistes Award at the Variety Club Showbusiness Awards ceremony. The whole band showed off their presenting skills on MTV and *The Pepsi Chart*, while individually Faye appeared on the Disney Channel, Lisa took over *SMTV* and H and Claire presented *Steps To The Stars*, the BBC talent show that became CBBC's most watched children's programme. Is there no end to the Steppers' skills?

The band had another massive hit in July with a double A-side single which brought together the beautiful ballad "When I Said Goodbye" and the Latino flavour of "Summer Of Love" in one of the best partnerships since apple crumble and custard (a Steps favourite!). In May and June Steps also completed another breathtaking 32-date tour which brought joy to everyone who got to see the stunning performances.

There's no doubting that Steps are Britain's premier pop band. Male or female, young or old, sensible or bonkers, everyone's a Steps fan.

And now you can get to know your favourite popsters even better because we're going to take you right behind the scenes to see Steps at

Steps In Private

work, rest, play, and best of all, doing the thing that they love more than anything else – touring.

The future's brighter than ever for Claire, Faye, H, Lisa and Lee, and you can bet that there are plenty more incredible tunes, top dance routines, and fantastic fun moments to come. So stay tuned and keep Stepping!

2 Claire In Private

Claire's hotel pseudonym:
Charlotte Angel. "I was trying to be a bit clever because it's like Charlie's Angels – Charlie is short for Charlotte!"

Up Close and Personal with Claire
All the band agree that Claire is one of the nicest girls that you could ever meet, and she's always there if the others need a chat on tour. She's probably the most reserved of the three wacky girls, and while she loves to party, she's also a bit of a homegirl at heart. So it comes as no surprise to discover that she often gets homesick while she's away on tour. As she says, "I still live with my family, so whenever we're in London working I get to go home to them every night, so I miss that. I speak to them every day, though. I miss my friends as well, but we always keep in touch so I don't get too lonely. I'm on my phone constantly!"

Steps In Private

So what does Claire do if she feels lonely while she's out on the road? "I just call Lisa," she says affectionately. "The other night we came in after a night out and she came into my room to have a gossip. When she said she was going to her room I didn't want her to go because I was feeling really lonely, so as I had two beds she ended up staying in my room. It wasn't like we even stayed up talking for ages, it was just nice to know that someone was there. As much as I like being on my own a lot, there are times when I feel like I need to have other people around me."

When Claire does fancy some time on her own, guess what she loves to do? Yep, she heads straight for the shops! "I like to go shopping on my own because for some reason it really helps to clear my head. I think because I'm looking at all the lovely clothes and shoes it takes my mind off everything else that's going on. I've also been going to the gym on my own to have a think about things, but it makes me ache so I don't go too often! I am very good at going swimming and for a steam, though! To be honest, whenever we have spare time I promise myself that I'm going to go to the gym, but I always end up going shopping instead."

H reckons that Claire's a bit too easily led when it comes to retail therapy. "She doesn't

Claire In Private

take much convincing to go shopping instead of to the gym," he laughs.

"The other day she said she was going to the gym and I said, 'Do you fancy going shopping instead?' and she was like, 'Yeeeeaaahhhh!' She bought a hat, two pairs of trainers and a top!"

"It's my mum's fault!" Claire says. "She's the ultimate bargain hunter and she taught me well. She can sniff out a bargain at one hundred paces and we used to go to Roman Road market [in London] and get millions of brilliant clothes really cheap. When I was younger Mum would put things on her credit card for me, and I'd work to pay her back. My mum's really good to go shopping with because she'll be like, 'Claire, do you really need that?' So she saves me money by stopping me from buying things. Mind you, I have to admit I usually buy them anyway!"

Another way Claire takes time off is by locking herself in her room and having a long bath and a chat to her family. "I like to be around people but I also like to have a bit of space and not have to worry about everybody else.

"I'll lie in a big bubble bath and phone my family and try and talk about normal stuff instead of pop stuff. It brings me back down to earth."

When Claire gets a couple of days off during the tour she heads straight home to see her

Steps In Private

family. The band had a day off after the Sheffield concerts, so Claire's mum and auntie came to see the show and she travelled back to London with them afterwards.

But even then there was no escape from eagle-eyed fans when she was spotted by a car full of Steps lovers while the trio were driving along the motorway. "I looked at the car next to us and all the people in it had all the Steps stuff on, the devil horns and t-shirts and everything." Claire laughs. "This one girl was leaning out of the window with a piece of paper and a pen trying to get my autograph. I couldn't believe it, it was so dangerous. I wouldn't recommend it!"

One way Claire doesn't pass the time, however, is by writing her diary! She promised herself that she'd record all her tour experiences and secrets in a diary which she bought especially to take away with her, but the truth is she hasn't put pen to paper since the first date in Glasgow. "I promised myself that I would keep it up to date, but the only thing I've written is about the plane journey to Glasgow on the first day. I'm *soooo* undisciplined. And I didn't even finish off the first day because I was supposed to go back and write about it after the first show had finished but I forgot! I really thought I'd write it every night so that I'd have something to look

Claire In Private

back on in years to come. Maybe I'll start again tonight? Then again, I said that yesterday . . . I think I might as well admit defeat and admit to myself that I'm just not going to write it. I'll have to read H's diary instead!"

Step Back in Time!
Being in Steps has been a crazy rollercoaster ride, but the fun is only just beginning for the glittery fivesome. Claire reflects on her life in Steps so far ...

How do you think you've changed since the beginning of Steps?
I don't think I've changed that much but I am a lot more confident than I was. I also find it easier to talk to people now, whereas before I used to wait for people to talk to me first because I was shy. I think I've learned to relax a bit as well, because in the beginning I was so determined to make it, and I wasn't going to stop until I got what I wanted. Then again, now I've got what I want I don't want to stop because I don't want to let it go, so maybe I haven't relaxed that much! I think we've all kept our feet on the ground really well though, and that's one of the reasons why we've been so successful.

Steps In Private

Did you ever expect the band to come this far?
No, never. I don't know what I expected to be honest. Because I'd been in a band before I kind of knew what to expect so I was a bit dubious to start off with. But then all of a sudden it just happened and the band really took off, and I still don't think it's really sunk in. I don't sit back and think, "Gosh, look how famous I am!" because I don't feel like that. I know we are famous but I still feel the same as I always did. It's a dream come true and I think we're all very, very lucky that we have achieved what we set out to achieve and ten times more.

What have been the best times for you so far?
It was really cool way, way back in the beginning. As much as it was hard work and we had to traipse up and down the country performing "5, 6, 7, 8" to clubs half full of people, we had a brilliant time and it was such a laugh. Also at the beginning so many people were cynical and people were knocking us, but now we can turn around and say "ha!" We've really proved ourselves and that feels great. We've learned who our true friends are and who we can and can't trust, and I think that's really important. One of the best things for me is that I can look around at the rest of the band and know that I can trust them and I've made four really brilliant friends.

Claire In Private

Is being in the band still as much fun as it always was?
Oh yeah. We have a laugh and I think we've got a new-found friendship where we know each other so well that it's really comfortable. We know what each other's faults and strengths are and none of it matters any more. We do go through some hard times sometimes, but if you can get through those and laugh, you can do anything. Sometimes we have days where we'll be in fits of giggles all day and no one should come anywhere near us because you can't get any sense out of us at all. I love it when all five of us are like that, it's fab. It's the funniest thing ever and it makes everything worthwhile.

How have you got through the hard times?
If bad things have happened in our personal lives or things have gone wrong work-wise, we've stuck together and been strong. I really do think that there aren't many bands around that have been together for the same amount of time as us that are still really good friends. We're so incredibly lucky.

What would people be surprised to discover about you after all this time?
That I'm actually really shy. People say to me, "How can you be shy when you get up in front of

Steps In Private

ten thousand people and sing?" but that's different, it's not really me. Well it is me, but it's the other side of me. It's like the minute I step up on stage I turn into a different person. I am actually really shy when I meet people that I don't know very well, which is why people sometimes think I'm quiet.

What's the weirdest rumour you've heard about yourself to date?
That I was going out with Lee, that one was around for ages. Another one was that I bought a £40,000 car because I was upset at being dumped. I mean, I did buy a car but it didn't cost £40,000 and it wasn't because I was dumped. It was because I wanted a new car!

How do you see the future of Steps?
I don't really like to look too far into the future because I think it's a bit dangerous. We're doing another album and hopefully that will do as well as the last two. I just want us to keep being happy and enjoying being with each other, and doing what we enjoy doing. I think when it gets too serious then it starts to get wrong, but thankfully we're still having fun.

Claire In Private

I Know Him (and Her) So Well!

The other Steppers reveal how their relationship with Claire has changed since the group first started out!

Lisa on Claire

For the first two years we were more like colleagues. We always got on and we never argued, but in the past year we've suddenly really bonded. Claire likes to come out more now whereas a year ago she'd be like, "How can you go out every night?" She couldn't quite understand the need to go out all the time, but I'm a bit of a party girl so I love it. And I couldn't really understand how she wanted to go to bed every night with a book! But now we've both changed a bit and she'll come out with me and we'll party together. We've grown really close and she's one of my best friends now. It's so good to have a best friend within a workplace because so often people who work together do just stay as colleagues, but I think we went past that a long time ago. We're really close now and it's lovely.

H on Claire

Claire hates it when I say this but when I first saw her I thought she was a lot older than she actually was – I thought she was about 28!

Steps In Private

She's never forgiven me for that. I always thought Claire was a lovely girl and I still do. When myself and Claire were filming *Steps To The Stars* in Manchester we became really close and got to know each other a lot better, and whenever we spend time together, just the two of us, we get on really well. That's when she's not on her phone. She's on the phone more than anyone else I know!

Faye on Claire
I think that when the group first got together we were all very excited about meeting each other and getting to know each other. Claire and I hit it off really well and I used to go and stay at her house a lot and we'd sit up talking for hours. We used to go shopping together all the time as well, but we can't do it as much now because we're much more recognisable if there are two of us. I miss being able to do silly things like that. These days Claire and I are like sisters, and we may not spend every waking moment with each other but I know that she's there for me. We're so relaxed with each other, it's a very natural friendship.

Lee on Claire
Claire and I didn't really get on that well in the beginning. Not that we hated each other or any-

Claire In Private

thing, we just didn't get on brilliantly. She was always, always late for everything and I used to be really hot on timekeeping. I always used to say to her, "Are you gonna be on time or what?" and we used to bicker about it. I've been late a few times myself since then though! In a way I was dreading me and Claire not getting on, but now we're really close and it's great. We've learned to respect each other and she's not even that late any more! And when she is, I've learned to deal with it because I've realised that it's not really that important.

Lee's lonely hearts ad for Claire!
"Clumsy Clara seeks doctor for emergency love treatment." She's so clumsy she needs someone to look after her!

3 The Backstage Secrets

Come with us as we take you on an exclusive journey backstage on the Steps tour. What do the band demand? How do they pass the time? How good are they at basketball?!?

What Goes On?

The backstage area of any concert venue is a hive of activity. The entire Steps tour is run like a military operation. Well, it has to be. There's always so much going on that if even one person wasn't doing their job properly the whole shebang could break down! Everyone who works on the shows is incredibly dedicated and skilled at their job. All the crew involved are old hands at touring, and have been responsible for making sure that a thousand tours before this one have run smoothly. All in all there are sixty people working on the tour, from the sound and lighting engineers to the set constructors. There's always a huge buzz with

The Backstage Secrets

people running around madly checking everything to ensure that absolutely nothing goes wrong. And thankfully 99 times out of 100, it doesn't!

The Soundcheck

Steps will generally arrive at a venue about two or three hours before the show starts, and the first thing they have to do is a soundcheck. This involves them taking to the stage while the arena is still completely empty and making sure that their microphones are working perfectly and they know where all the trap doors and props are situated.

H also has to do his flying practice (usually when the girls are practising their breathtaking ballad "I Know Him So Well"). "I have to check that everything's OK for my flying every night because it can be extremely dangerous if everything isn't set up perfectly," H says sounding serious for once! "I make sure that all my wires are OK and there's no danger of it going wrong. Do I get nervous about it? Well, the performance is actually really technical and there are so many things that could go wrong that it can be a bit nerve-racking. Thankfully nothing has gone wrong yet, but sometimes when I'm up there above everyone I look down and realise

Steps In Private

what I'm doing and I get a bit worried. But I enjoy it as well.

It's an amazing feeling to be swooping across the arena!"

It's Chow Time

After the soundcheck Steps have one thing on their minds – dinner! And Home Cookin', a catering company which stays with the band throughout the tour, are always on hand to provide delicious hot meals and tempting puddings. The Home Cookin' gang set up in the catering area at each venue every afternoon, so by the time the band arrive they have a wide choice of meals, drinks and incredible cakes!

"Home Cookin' do some really great healthy food, but they also do some really naughty, lovely meals!" says Faye.

"We have roast lunches on Sundays and puddings to die for – it's just wonderful! There's always a really good choice, and a healthy choice if we want it. But I don't always want it when I see what's on offer!"

Lisa's been eating as healthily as possible to keep her strength up. "I don't really eat much junk food, I prefer to eat healthily because it makes me feel so much better, especially when we're working so hard. I often have something

The Backstage Secrets

like mashed potato with vegetables. Luckily I love vegetables so it's easy for me to be healthy."

Lee is similar to Lisa in that nine times out of ten he goes for the healthy option. But even he's been finding it hard to resist the gorgeous puddings. "I've been eating so much!" he laughs. "I've been eating a lot of steak and chicken, but my favourite thing is the apple crumble and custard. It's so delicious. And I burn all the puddings off in the gym and on stage anyway, so I'm allowed them! But I do also have a lot of fruit and salads, and all of the band drink lots and lots of water. You need to do that because you sweat a lot on stage. Water's really good for you because it rehydrates you and it also clears you out."

H says he's been trying really hard to follow Lee and Lisa's good examples, but finds it really hard when he's tempted by all these incredible edibles. "I usually eat things like cake and pizza, but I've tried to eat as well as possible on this tour. But it's so ridiculously difficult when the caterers do all these amazing puddings. As soon as I see these gorgeous gooey messes I can't help eating them! But I do have vegetables and stuff sometimes, honestly!"

Even self-confessed junk food addict Claire has been eating her fair share of fruit and veg on the tour to keep her super-fit during

Steps In Private

what can sometimes be a very demanding schedule.

"I have eaten a bit of junk, but I've only eaten one McDonalds – which is really good . . . for me!

"I've eaten chicken almost every night, and I've been eating vegetables as well. And some nights I've been having fruit for pudding instead of sticky cakes and things, which I feel very proud about! I think Lisa's healthy ways are rubbing off on me!"

Claire agrees with Lisa that you can feel a difference when you eat well. "You definitely have more energy, but I think you have to get a balance. If I want chips I eat them because that's what I fancy. Mind you, the other night I ordered some from room service in a hotel and they brought me enough to feed about five people. It was mad."

Claire also has a bit of a strange theory about why she loves junk food so much. "When my mum was pregnant with me she craved cheeseburgers so badly that she would even eat them cold, and I think it's been passed on because I absolutely love them! I also love bread, which she craved, so maybe that's been passed on too? My sister loves satsumas and my mum craved them when she was pregnant with my sister, so I'm sure

The Backstage Secrets

that's what it is. I know it sounds mad, but it's true!"

When They Say Hello!

Steps do meet and greets before most shows. This is where they get to say hello to competition winners and other lucky fans! Tonight there are twelve competition winners sitting nervously around tables in a private room backstage at Newcastle Arena waiting to meet their idols. "I'm going to be sick, I'm *sooooooo* excited!" says one clutching her hands together nervously. "I'm not gonna know what to say. I won't be able to speak!" says another. They all chat at nineteen to the dozen trying to calm their nerves as they constantly look at the door, waiting as patiently as possible for the band to walk in.

At the very back of the room a mother sits with her six-year-old daughter Charlotte. It's hard to know who's more excited about the prospect of meeting Steps – Charlotte or her mum! "I've been waiting all day!" mum laughs.

"I think they're such a lovely band. I won the competition on the radio. I was calling up on my mobile and my home phone at the same time.

"You had to be the hundredth person to call in so I kept having to put the number on re-dial

Steps In Private

and eventually we got through and here we are. I still can't quite believe it!"

Suddenly the band burst through the door with big waves and shouts of "hello!" Faye, Claire, H, Lisa and Lee all smile broadly as they start making their way around the room. But instead of leaping out of their seats and running over to the band, everyone looks on in awe, too stunned to move. It's not until the band split up and approach the tables that all of the competition winners start to speak. But once they do, there's no stopping them!

"I like your hair Lisa, will you sign this?"

"H, will you leave a message on my answer phone for me?"

"I love your dreadlocks Faye!"

The band work their way around each table in a flurry of kisses and cheery conversations. One girl begins crying and Lee gives her a hug "I'm sorry," she sniffs. "I just can't believe that I'm standing next to you. You're so gorgeous!"

While all the other competition winners are in full flow, Charlotte is dumbstruck. She sits and looks intently at her Steps postcard as the band walk towards her table. She flicks her eyes towards the band in disbelief, and then asks her mum if it's really them. H approaches her table and says hello, and her eyes widen while she summons up the confidence to say hello back.

The Backstage Secrets

H, being H, breaks the tension by lifting her out of her seat and twirling her around. She dissolves into fits of giggles and at last manages to say a timid hello to her favourite Stepper.

The band stay and chat for ages, but time is tight and they have to go off and get themselves ready for the concert. They all shout goodbye and blow kisses as they head for their dressing rooms, and the fans carry on waving and grinning long after the band have gone.

The fans exchange stories, show off autographs, and discuss who their favourite Steps member was, while two girls argue about whether H or Lee is the best-looking Steps guy. One boy looks as if he's about to cry. "I just can't believe I've met her," he says half-smiling, half-tearful as he stares at his signed picture of Claire. "She was so lovely to me, and even more beautiful in the flesh. This really is the best day of my life." And one that he'll no doubt remember for the rest of his life!

Steps Have a Ball!

When they've got some time before the shows, the Steppers often take the opportunity to get together and get competitive! Lee always brings a football with him on tour, and the rest of the band like to join him for a kickabout or shoot

Steps In Private

some hoops if there's a net around. If the band want to chill out before the hecticness of the show and there's an area of tarmac around, there's no stopping them . . .

We join them as they slam, dribble and shoot like pros. Faye is first to take to the makeshift court alongside the crew. She grabs the ball and dribbles it towards the hoop, where she scores a goal the first time she shoots.

H and Lee are next to emerge from the catering area and join her. Lee swiftly nicks the ball and slams it in the net. "Show off!" Faye hollers at him, laughing.

H dives in to take control of the ball, but what he didn't realise was that Claire has also come out to join in the game. She ducks in and before he even realises that she's done a smooth move on him she's heading off in the other direction with the ball. "I'm useless at basketball," she says making her first attempt to score a goal. "I was in the netball team at school, but I'm not very good at this." She misses, but second time around she is successful and punches the air in celebration.

Next it's Faye's turn to score again. Is she a bit of a basketball whiz? "No, I wouldn't say I'm a whiz!" she smiles. "It's just a really nice way to chill out and it's something different to do. It's good to get some fresh air in your lungs and it gets you all pumped up for the show. You do

The Backstage Secrets

spend a lot of time inside, so if we get the chance we'll go outside."

Lisa is the only Stepper missing out on this evening's basketball fun. She's inside doing a phone interview for a magazine that wants to know all her fashion secrets!

Steps fans never miss a trick, and before you can say "Blimey, there's Steps playing basketball!" a group of eagle-eyed fans have walked around the outside of the arena and positioned themselves where they have a perfect view of the band at play. The entire area surrounding the band is cordoned off by a wire fence, but as Steps continue their match, word spreads and the small group grows bigger and bigger until it becomes a crowd.

They all shout to the band and beg them to come and say hello, so one by one the Steppers approach the fence and collect their presents and cards and sign things for them. One fan passes over a huge cake he's brought for H's birthday, while Lee and H make sure that they don't turn their backs on the crowd for a second. Every time they do the fans are grabbing and pinching their bums, and one grabs H so hard he's convinced he's going to have a bruise the next day. "That really hurt, I'm gonna be scarred for life!" he says with a pained expression on his face.

Steps In Private

"Blimey, they're not shy, listen to them!" says Lee as they shout saucy comments in his direction.

One hardcore group of fans, who are sporting homemade t-shirts with huge 'S's on the front, begin to climb up the fence so that they can get a better look at the band. "Be careful," says a concerned Claire, "we don't want you hurting yourselves and missing the show." The fans duly climb down and continue watching the band's every move. They cheer every time someone scores and get their cameras out so that they can catch the moment on film. The fans go wild when Claire turns the tables on them and grabs the photographer's camera and starts taking pictures of them. "Smile!" she giggles. "It's your turn to be photographed!"

H laughs and then looks confused. "I've lost my mobile phone," he says. "I put it down somewhere for safekeeping but I can't remember where." He looks for ages and occasionally throws his hands into the air in despair. "It must be here somewhere." In the end he gets Lee to call his number so that he can follow the ring. "I've got it!" he grins, and holds it in the air triumphantly before putting it back down in the same spot and continuing to play.

There's no dragging Claire away from the

The Backstage Secrets

game, especially as one of the dancers keeps trying to grab her so that they can rehearse a particularly difficult dance move.

One of the other dancers has been taken ill, meaning that this guy will have to lift Claire on his own during the "Better The Devil You Know" routine that night. "I don't want to do it, I'm terrified," she explains, bouncing the ball in the opposite direction from him. "It's scary enough as it is, let alone when one of the dancers is missing. That's why I'm running away from him!" she laughs mischievously.

In the end there is no avoiding him. "It's now or never," he tells her carrying her off. In the end she gives up and agrees to rehearse the move, and a look of relief sweeps across her face when she realises that it's not as difficult as she first thought.

Later that night they do the move for real. On stage. In front of ten thousand people. Claire's face is flashed onto the big screen and she looks a tad apprehensive, but they pull it off perfectly, and Claire manages to smile all the way through despite wobbling ever so slightly when the dancer lowers her back onto the stage. Success!

The basketball game comes to an end when the band begin to filter inside to get ready. "It's nearly showtime!" H beams as he waves goodbye to the fans.

Steps In Private

A Peek Inside the Dressing Rooms

Along with catering, the dressing rooms are where everything happens before a gig. Make-up is perfected, hair is coiffured and voices are warmed up. For an hour and a half before each show the dressing rooms are where the band gather to collect their thoughts and psyche themselves up for the hectic show ahead.

While the band do generally have light-up mirrors and comfy sofas in their dressing rooms, not all dressing rooms are glamorous. In fact, some can be downright dodgy with nasty decor and 70s furniture! But the band always liven things up by making sure they add their own personal touches and have a stereo handy.

Claire has just bought a super-swanky minidisc player so she can listen to her favourite tunes.

The album of the moment for the girls' dressing room is Sisqo's *Unleash The Dragon*, although they've also been getting retro with Michael Jackson's *Bad* album.

"You should hear us singing along, it's hilarious!" laughs Claire.

The boys get down and get funky with H's ghetto blaster, and the preferred choice of music in their dressing room is Britney Spears' most recent album, which H has been playing non-stop.

The Backstage Secrets

Needless to say, the girls all share one dressing room, while Lee and H share another. They're generally next door to each other so that they can all pop in and out while they're getting ready. They all find that it helps to keep them calm if they've got each other to talk to, although Lisa reckons that H always goes into their dressing room at just the wrong time. "It's always when we're in the middle of getting undressed! The boys are supposed to be banned so that we can be all girly, but he practically lives in our room. I think he just wants attention if Lee's busy doing other things," she laughs.

Unlike certain barmy popsters who will request bowls of sweets with the brown ones removed (yes, really) or mega-expensive caviar, Steps' dressing room requirements are pretty straightforward.

Water, water and more water! They also have a bowl of fruit, cranberry and orange juice, crisps, chocolate, and a cheeky bottle of wine, "For when we come off stage!" Lisa explains.

They also have a big candle that they burn to chill out, some joss sticks to relax them, a box of tissues and a toiletry box which is placed in their room each night by Dawn, the wardrobe lady. It's packed full of gorgeous smelly things like deodorant, make-up remover, cotton wool

Steps In Private

and shower gel so that they can be zingy and fresh when they leap on stage!

H is particularly taken with the mini-toothbrushes. "They've even got our names on them!" he says, astonished. The boys also have a selection of teddies and gifts from fans in their room, while the girls put up pictures that the fans have drawn of them.

The girls always do their own hair and make-up before a concert. It's something that they've learned to do to perfection over the past three years. As Lisa explains, "We've always had make-up artists, and we've picked up so many tips off them that we can just as easily do it ourselves now – so we do! We've learned what suits us and what doesn't, how to make our make-up stay on on stage, all of those things. We can do it really quickly now as well because we've practised so much. We still have hair and make-up artists if we're doing a big photo shoot, but while it's lovely to be pampered like that, there's no point in us having someone with us all the time when we can do it ourselves."

"It's the same with our hair," Claire continues. "When we first started out we'd spend hours making sure that our hair looked perfect, but now we all find it really easy to do. My sister's a hairdresser as well so she's taught me loads,

The Backstage Secrets

she's brilliant. In fact, my sister's even given me hair dye to bring with me so that I can do my roots on tour. It's so much easier than having to search out a hairdresser."

"Claire helps me with my hair if I'm having a nightmare as well," Lisa says. "She's dead good at it.

"She twists it around all over the place, sprays it with hairspray, and it's done. Magic! But when it comes to getting the colour done I go to the same place as H, Andrew Jose in London. I love having it done red because I'm known for being a bit feisty and I think it suits my fiery personality!"

Faye says that because she had dreadlocks put in for the tour, she can also do her hair pretty quickly. "I got it done at Children Of Vision in Notting Hill, which is where I usually have it done," she explains. "I went there a couple of weeks before the tour. I had to have my roots done first and then it took about four hours to do the extensions, so I was in there for about seven hours in all! Luckily I had my phone so I called all my friends and family. I also had magazines and I was playing my new Muppets game on my Gameboy."

So just how did Faye decide what to do with her hair this time around? "Well, I was going to go for normal plaits and get it braided but I was

Steps In Private

worried that I'd be constantly whacking myself in the eye on stage," she confides.

"I thought that the fans would expect me to do something drastic so I decided to have dreadlocks like last time!

"All the colours are my favourite colours. Turquoise blue is my absolute favourite colour so I had that put in, then I had pink to soften it up, and then we popped a bit of orange in there to make it look pretty! So now I'm rainbow bright!"

But despite it taking so long to do, Faye has a very good reason for taking the extensions out as soon as the tour is finished. "I'm going on holiday straight away to relax so I want to be able to swim and stuff without worrying about my hair. I can't go on holiday and not swim. And there's no way I can swim with dreadlocks!"

When it comes to make-up, all the girls love using a real mixture of products, but their favourite range of the moment is the cool Ruby and Millie collection. They've just been given some free products, and they're feeling very happy indeed! "They've been really good to us," says Faye. "They've got some really amazing colours and we've been experimenting with them all. And Boots gave us some free stuff as well. It's all been very exciting!"

The Backstage Secrets

And girls being girls, they all borrow each other's make-up. "Why just use your own when you've got three lots to play with?" Claire says.

Stage make-up can play havoc with your skin, and Faye's face has been feeling a bit sore of late. "Some of the make-up we use is really heavy because it's made specially for stage use," she says. "And obviously we have to put a new lot on every night, and then take it all off again. And if we have to do a photo shoot during the day we have to put another lot on! After all that your skin is bound to get irritated." Faye's been applying aloe vera gel to her face which is helping to soothe it.

"And of course the other trick is not to wear make-up when you're not working. You have to give your skin a rest and make sure that you look after it"

Lisa agrees. "I'm lucky because our make-up artist says that my make-up stays on really well so I don't have to keep reapplying it too often. But I always make sure that I take it off before I go to bed and I moisturise.

Never forget to moisturise!"

The boys' drill is a tad more straightforward than the girls, as Lisa explains. "It's so funny because all you can hear from our room is us warbling and asking each other for make-up advice and about how we should do our hair.

Steps In Private

But the boys' room is much quieter, and they don't take nearly as long to get ready."

H agrees. "Me and Lee usually start getting ready when the girls are already half-ready, getting their make-up on and doing all sorts of girlie things! All we have to do is our hair and we're ready to go, so we sit around and have a chat and relax with our lovely candle instead."

The dressing rooms are always manic with people coming in and out, having meetings with the band mid-preparation, making sure they have everything they need, letting them know of any last-minute changes, or just popping their heads round the corner to say good luck. However, it's not as though just anyone gets the chance to see the band while they're getting ready. Security is always tight, and generally a bodyguard will sit outside to ensure that no undesirables manage to go a-knocking on the band's doors!

About half an hour before the band go on stage, their first outfit of the night comes off the rails in the dressing rooms and onto the band! Steps wardrobe lady Dawn comes up to the dressing rooms to make sure that there are no broken zips or missing buttons. "The costumes are checked constantly to make sure that they're OK," says Lisa. "You can never check them enough.

The Backstage Secrets

"It would be slightly off-putting if you were dancing and all of a sudden your button flew off or your zip came undone!"

"We always get dressed for the opening number in our rooms," says Lee. "But we do all our other costume changes in a room at the side of the stage which we run into as soon as we come off stage. It's always such a rush, it's mad, but thankfully we have costume people who make sure that everything's laid out ready for us, and none of us have had to go on stage half-naked yet. Mind you, I wouldn't be surprised if I went into the changing room one day to find that H had hidden all my clothes for a laugh. I'd kill him!"

Thankfully there have been no total costume disasters and no one has revealed themselves to the audience as yet! Lisa puts that down to the clever way the show is timed. "We have a lot more time to get changed in between than we did on the last tour," she explains. "We've split the show so that someone is always on stage, meaning that the rest of us have time to get our outfits on and make sure they're properly done up. I've only had one thing go wrong and that was when the side of my top came undone, but I just carried on singing and cunningly did it up as I was dancing!

"Can you imagine if it had totally fallen off? The papers would have had a field day!"

Steps In Private

"I do worry about that," smiles Claire. "There's always this danger that your trousers are suddenly going to fall down, and it's not like no one would notice. We've got ten thousand people out there watching and we'd never live it down!"

Wardrobe lady Dawn also helps the guys and gals to fit their headsets and earpieces, which help them hear the backing tracks when the audiences are screaming like mad.

"If we didn't wear earpieces we'd never be able to hear what we were singing along to because the audiences are so incredibly loud!" says H.

When their costumes are all sorted out, it's time for the band to do their pre-show warm-up, and each person has their own ritual. All of the band do an essential vocal warm-up to ensure that their voice is well prepared for a rigorous night's singing! Claire always has a hot drink and covers herself in body glitter (though not at the same time, obviously), H runs around talking to everyone and laughing, Lisa hugs everyone, Lee does some last-minute press-ups to get himself hyped up, and Faye always makes one last phone call. Then they all leave their dressing rooms together and go and chat to the dancers so that everyone can fire each other up. Then it's time to hit the stage...

The Backstage Secrets

After the Show . . .

The second the show ends there are people waiting in the wings to provide each member of Steps with a personalised white towelling bath robe to keep them warm as they run outside and get straight in their Galaxy Space Cruisers. The engines are already running so that the band can zoom off before the fans can leave the show and make their way round to the back of the arena. This is to prevent accidents, as it would be practically impossible for the vehicles to leave the arena if a crowd had gathered around the backstage gates. "We'd love to be able to stay and chat to people straight after the show, but it's just too dangerous," says Lisa. "If you can imagine ten thousand people all wanting to say hello to you and get autographs, unfortunately it just can't be done. It's so much safer for us to leave straight away because that way people are happy to go home if they know that we've already left the arena."

The vehicles then take the fivesome straight back to their hotel where they go straight to their rooms for a shower or bath, "So we can wash all our glitter off!" laughs Faye.

And needless to say, if people are in the lift when Steps jump in fresh from a performance, the band end up getting some pretty strange looks. "It's funny because if you get into a lift in

Steps In Private

a hotel immediately after a show and you're sweating and your hair and make-up are all over the place and you're wearing your dressing gown, people look astounded. I'm sure they expect you to look glamorous all the time, but how can you look glamorous when you've been dancing and sweating on stage for the last hour and a half and you're wrapped in a bathrobe? The answer is you can't. But we do our best, sweedie . . . !"

4 Lee In Private

Lee's hotel pseudonym:
Dick Dastardly. "I've had to stop using it now though because it was too cartoony and obvious."

Up Close and Personal with Lee
Lee is the Stepper most likely to make sure that everyone's organised and knows what's going on when they're on tour. He loves touring as much as the rest of the band and says that he doesn't get homesick at all, which makes being away from home easier for him. "I've lived away from my family for almost seven years and I'm quite independent, so I don't miss home very much. I keep in touch with my friends when I'm on the road anyway. Also, I don't own my own home like the rest of the guys yet. I think everyone else misses their houses but I don't have one to miss at the moment. I think when I get my own place I'll miss it because I'll be buying

Steps In Private

nice things for it and it'll really be mine, but at the moment I'm fine."

In fact, instead of missing his mates, Lee thinks that touring is actually a brilliant time for him to catch up with old friends.

"It's cool because you get to see all the people you know around the country that you don't usually get to see.

"It's funny because when I was younger I used to really enjoy being on my own, but I enjoy being around people now. I enjoy good company."

Lee also has a little friend that he carries around with him that keeps him company. "I've got a little mascot that I take with me. It's an ickle beanie cow, and I call it ickle cow!"

Of course, the gym is the place that Lee heads to when he needs to take time out on his own away from it all. "I use all my energy in the gym. Not only does it make me healthy and give me a better body, but it's also my step away from it all.

"It's my escape from the world. In a way the gym is the place where I can gather my thoughts. If you want to get deep about it, I guess it's where I'm most at one with myself.

"I'm doing my stretching and the right breathing and I'm concentrating really hard. No one else is around me and no one is bothering me or asking me for anything. It's my time."

Lee In Private

Lisa says that Lee's incredibly disciplined when it comes to working out. "He gets into his gym mode and he has his breakfast at nine and goes to the gym at half ten. Then he showers and he's ready for work. He has a routine which he follows for the whole tour. It's very impressive!"

So when did Lee's love of the gym begin? "I started going to the gym when I was fifteen because I was very sporty and active and I never really put any weight on. I was very thin, I was like a stick insect, and I started going to the gym to give me a shape. I didn't go to become big and muscly or anything special, it was literally to stop me looking so thin! But then I started to really enjoy it. It's a bit of a mind and body thing for me. I actually feel better when I go to the gym."

Step Back in Time!
Being in Steps has been a crazy rollercoaster ride, but the fun is only just beginning for the glittery fivesome. Lee reflects on his life in Steps so far . . .

How do you think you've changed since the beginning of Steps?
I honestly don't think we have that much. Obviously we've become wiser and we know

Steps In Private

more about the business and people are listening to us a bit more which is nice. As people we've still got the same ambitions and the same goals. We're still sticking at what we want and that's just to be successful, stay on top, and enjoy the tours and stuff. We haven't become arrogant gits or anything. We're probably a bit more tired then we used to be, but it's for a very good reason!

Did you ever expect the band to come this far?
I think we were all a bit dubious and a bit concerned about how it was all going to go, but once things started they just kept getting better and better. But at the end of the day, we've done so well now and we've worked so hard for what we've got that I just kind of think, "How did we get here?" I think we're surprised every day, but at the same time we don't get time to sit back and actually look at it because we're always so busy. We saw a *Top Of The Pops* half-hour special on Steps a little while ago and it was made up of lots of interviews and the songs and all the things we've done. I was looking at it thinking "wow" and it really hit me how much we've accomplished. It was always our dream to do this well, but I don't think we can believe that we're selling out all the arenas and selling mil-

Lee In Private

lions of records. It's just incredible, it's all we ever wanted.

What have been the best times for you so far?
I loved it when we got the BRIT award because it was an achievement award, not a category award. It was just saying that we deserved an award because we'd done so well, and that was an incredible feeling. I felt like we were really showing people who had doubted us. We've proved so many people wrong and I like that a lot! I loved presenting the *Smash Hits* awards as well. The first year we did it we were opening the show as a support act, the second year we ended the show with "Tragedy", and the third year we presented the whole thing! It's amazing to watch it grow. There have been a lot of highlights – travelling the world hasn't been bad either! I can't actually remember any really, really negative times. At the end of the day we enjoy performing and we enjoy seeing the fans, so we're constantly having a good time.

Is being in the band still as much fun as it always was?
Yes, I really do think it is. I guess it's become more of a business because at first we were doing it for fun and we weren't really sure where we were going or what we were doing. Then all

Steps In Private

of a sudden it kicked in and everything took off in a big way and we're having dolls made of us! There are even Steps karaoke machines coming out this Christmas! It is more of a business, but that doesn't mean it's less fun. We're still having the time of our lives.

How have you got through the hard times?
By being together. Of course there are some difficult things like missing your family and friends, and when we're travelling a lot we can get very tired which can be a bit difficult. And of course, we've all had things to deal with in our personal lives along the way, and it's not like you can just decide to take two weeks off, because life goes on and there are four other people to think about. But we're all there for each other, and that gets us through everything.

What would people be surprised to discover about you after all this time?
That I'm a big softie. And I'm not a big partygoer, I'm just as happy staying at home and relaxing as I am going to a glamorous party. Everyone has a dream about making loads of money or doing the right job, but my dream is to be like my parents. I want to be very grounded and very homely and have a lovely girl that will be there for me always, and I'll

Lee In Private

give them everything I can and respect them and be there for them and live my life for them. If I'm doing that and I'm a star, great. But if I'm not, so what? As long as I've got that I'll be happy.

[Something else you'll be surprised to know is that Lee has a tattoo! It's one of the best kept secrets in pop but now all is revealed and here Lee tells us all about it!]

It's a sun and moon design and if you look closely it looks like the moon is about to kiss the sun.

I got it done in Venice Beach in Los Angeles. Faye came with me when I had it done for moral support! I designed it myself with the guy in the tattoo parlour. It's like day becoming night and it means 'timeless'. [So there you have it!]

What's the weirdest rumour you've heard about yourself to date?
There hasn't been anything too weird to be honest. I loved it when I did a shoot for the women's magazine *Cosmopolitan*. I was the first male to be on the cover for sixteen years and the papers were really positive towards me and I felt like all my time in the gym had paid off. I like anything that's nice because the press can be really negative sometimes. I love it when the press write about us selling out massive arena

Steps In Private

tours because people may think that they're rumours, but they're actually true!

How do you see the future of Steps?
H and I sing a song on tour called "Things Can Only Get Better", and I think things are getting better and better for us every day. It's a bigger game, it's a bigger adventure, but luckily we haven't got bigger heads to go with it. We're not going to change too much but we're going to try new things and hope that it opens more doors for us.

I Know Him (and Her) so Well!
The other Steppers reveal how their relationship with Lee has changed since the group first started out!

Lisa on Lee
Lee and I have always got on well and Lee's a very good listener. I know that I can go to him if I've got any kind of problem. Anything I tell him won't go any further. And he'll come to me and talk about things as well, we can have really brilliant chats. I think we've always had a really good friendship because he's always been very grown up and he's really got his head screwed on. We all still get on remarkably well consider-

Lee In Private

ing that we've been together constantly for the past three years.

Faye on Lee
To start with I found it really hard to read him, but now I've got to know him really well. He's someone you can really trust, he's very loyal and has a really calm air around him. You will always feel safe around Lee. If something's troubling him I can see the little signs, and if he's happy I can tell a mile off. He's also like the ear of the band if you want to get something off your chest. He's like a sponge, he takes everything in and keeps it to himself.

H on Lee
Me and Lee became friends quickly because we lived together when the band first started out. I bought a gym for the house and me and Lee used to work out on that, and then we joined a gym together. We also used to catch the train together to work and stuff, so we got to be mates from the beginning. And we still share dressing rooms now so we still spend a lot of time together – especially while we're waiting for the girls to get ready! Lee's always been a really good person to talk to as well because he's very level-headed, and while I've got friends outside the band that I can confide in, I talk to Lee a lot as well.

Steps In Private

Claire on Lee
Me and Lee are friends and we always will be, but we got on each other's nerves a bit in the beginning! He hated the fact that I wasn't very good with my timekeeping. Also, he's the eldest and I'm the youngest so it became a brother/sister kind of relationship. The only other person that I feel the same way I do about Lee is my sister, she's the only other person that can wind me up the same way he does. It's a good thing in a way because it means that we can wind each other up and we'll forget about it five minutes later. There's a real affection there between us, we've kind of chilled out and we don't let things bother us. I know I can go and talk to him and he'll give me a hug if I need it. I don't talk about my feelings that much, but I know that whatever happens I can always go to him if I need to.

Faye's lonely hearts ad for Lee
"Tall, dark, handsome, mysterious, modest but adventurous male seeks feisty, interesting, sporty female!" Lee needs a girl that can keep him on his toes!

5 It's Showtime!

Step To It!

Steps rehearsed for the record-breaking *Steptacular* tour in two different venues. They started out in London, where they stayed in a huge studio for three weeks perfecting the dance routines and making sure that everything ran smoothly. Next they moved on to Windsor, where the entire set was built to enable them to do a full run-through.

Rehearsals are always an incredibly busy time, but when you've got a single to record at the same time things can get decidedly hectic! "We were actually recording 'Summer Of Love', which we performed in the show, during rehearsals," Faye reveals.

"We needed to have a proper finished version done before we started the tour, so what with that and rehearsals we had quite a few late nights. But we got everything done and we didn't even get behind. I think the only thing that was a bit late was the set. I think we did really

Steps In Private

well, and all the hard work was definitely worth it."

Too right! The shows were heart-stopping, tear-jerking, jaw-dropping, foot-stomping affairs, and above all, they were tons of fun!

The *Steptacular* tour was the biggest pop tour the UK has ever seen. But do they love touring as much as we love watching them perform? You bet!

What's your favourite thing about touring?

Claire: Getting up on stage every night and doing what we're here to do. We all love dancing and we all love singing, it's what we're all about. Also we get to have all the dancers and our management around us, and I know it sounds a bit cheesy but it's like a great big family. It's a really brilliant atmosphere.

Faye: It's my favourite part of being in Steps.

You get to dance and sing every night, and you get to socialise and have time off during the day so that you can go shopping.

And you get to see your family and friends around the country. I love everything about it!

Lisa: Touring is the reason I actually joined Steps. I was a professional singer and dancer

It's Showtime!

before but I was on the cabaret level, so I wanted to step it up a gear and do it in the music industry. It's always such a huge buzz when you're travelling the country entertaining people and having a laugh. I'd like to be on tour all year round, I'd be quite happy to do it.

H: We usually spend a lot of time doing TV and radio interviews, and while we have a fantastic time doing that, the reason we got into this business is to perform. So to be on stage performing in front of all our fans feels absolutely fantastic.

Lee: To have that full audience in front of you getting the real live event is so special. You get an immediate reaction and it's so incredible to look out and see everyone enjoying themselves and know that you're a part of that. It's also great to get to see the fans and spend some time with our families.

What's your favourite part of the show?

Faye: I think mine has to be when us three girls sing "I Know Him So Well". We really get the chance to show off our voices. We're all crooners at heart and it's like we're having a karaoke session on stage!

Steps In Private

Claire: I love performing that as well, we get to really belt it out.
I look forward to it every night!

Lee: I like doing my song "Come On Get Together" because it's so different to the rest of the show and also I co-wrote it. I enjoy doing the new stuff, and I like doing my duet of "Things Can Only Get Better" with H. I think it's surprised a lot of people.

H: Mine's the bit where I fly, without a doubt. Flying is something that I've always dreamed of doing. I always loved Peter Pan as a kid, and I went to see the musical in New York on Broadway which was so fantastic it inspired me to do it myself!

Lisa: I love it when H flies as well. He rehearsed for ages to do it and he does loads of flips and stuff, which I think is really clever. But my fave bit has to be my solo because it's been an ambition of mine to perform a song that I wrote myself.

What do you always pack to bring with you on tour?

Lisa: One of my Rugrats, usually my Baby Dill that Claire bought me. I also need to have my

It's Showtime!

phone with me at all times, and my Gameboy, CD player and my songwriting book. I always make sure I've got loads of different means of entertainment so if we do have a couple of hours where we're a bit bored we've got something to do. And of course I have enough clothes for a month. We get our clothes washed in the hotels so luckily we don't have to take too much stuff. Mind you, Claire still brings quite a lot.

Claire: It's true, I bring everything! I take everything I own with me.

I've got a big case with all my clothes in it, a smaller case with all my shoes in it, and another case with my washbag and my toiletries and my hair stuff in it.

Then I've got an extra little bag for all my make-up, and a big handbag that's got my CD player and stuff in it, and then I've got my little handbag. And I also pick up a few carrier bags along the way so I end up with tons of stuff!

Faye: I always have my full make-up kit, my Discman and my Gameboy. I'm not a great reader but I do pick up the odd magazine along the way. And of course I always bring some clothes!

I also have to take a teddy. I've got this little cuddly toy dog that I take with me. On the first tour I bought this huge dog, but since then I've

Steps In Private

bought every size in the collection down to the little one, and the little one is the one that comes with me now.

H: I have to have my CD player and my big ghetto blaster which we have in the dressing room so that we can do a vocal warm-up before we go on stage – lalalalala! I also take my diary with me so that I can write the events of every night down. I'm very good at keeping it up to date. I've also started taking my sit-up machine everywhere with me because I've started using it again. No one's actually seen the results yet because I've still got a bit of work to do. But all will be revealed!

Lee: I don't actually take that much. I have a few clothes, a Dictaphone in case I get any ideas for songs, some gym equipment because I like to work out every morning, my games console to chill out with and my mobile phone. Just essential stuff, really.

The brilliant thing is that if you're on tour and don't have enough clothes you can always go shopping when you get a bit of time off!

Has anything gone horribly wrong on the tour?!

Faye: I got my heel caught in the trap door which was a bit unnerving! I thought I was going

It's Showtime!

to have to take my shoes off and carry on the show in bare feet but luckily I yanked it out.

H: I went the wrong way during a dance routine for "Last Thing On My Mind". I was so busy waving at the fans that I forgot what I was doing and went completely the wrong way. I stuck out like a sore thumb! Claire was howling with laughter!

Claire: I was wetting myself. We wear these earpieces so we can't hear anything but the backing music, but I must have laughed really loud because all the dancers turned around and looked at me!

Lisa: One night I nearly injured myself really badly. When I do my solo I perform my song which I've written with Ray Hedges, and at the end of the song they open trap doors so that the boys can come down for the next number. So there are massive holes in the stage and I completely forgot they were there! I was strutting along in my massive platforms as usual, and literally just missed falling down. It could have been really dangerous. I was terrified, I felt really funny afterwards. I don't think too many people noticed.

Then the other night I was feeling a bit tired and I was trying my hardest not to yawn. But as

Steps In Private

I was trying to stifle a yawn the cameramen did a close up of my face across three massive screens and my nose was twitching and my nostrils were all flared! I dread to think what I looked like.

Lee: I had a bit of a scare during "Better The Devil You Know". When we come up from underneath the stage on a platform the pyros, fireworks-type things, go off. One night I was standing there and one landed on my head! Then the next night all the sparks from another one landed on my head.

I was there trying to do the dance routine and shaking my head about all over the place so the sparks wouldn't set fire to my hair. I must have looked ridiculous!

The show must go on!

Did you miss out on the show of a lifetime? Never fear, we'll take you there! Read on to get a taste of just how brilliant the shows were . . . Picture the scene. A massive arena, ten thousand excited fans, a night they'll never forget. All in all Steps played a record-breaking 32 shows during the tour, and each and every one was a huge success with the band going wild and the audiences going even wilder!

Crowds would queue excitedly outside the

It's Showtime!

arenas practically all day just so that they could be the first through the doors and soak up the incredible atmosphere before the show began. As soon as the doors opened, despite already having been allocated seats, everyone would run like the wind and find their position before nipping back out to the foyer to take their pick of the fab range of merchandise which was on offer.

T-shirts were chosen, programmes were pored over and posters were snapped up. The most popular things to wear during the show were the huge glittery "Deeper Shade Of Blue" Steps hands, flashing devil horns, and shimmery silver deeley-boppers which were everywhere you looked! What an amazing sight!

The audiences were a real mixture of people, from the under-fives to fun-loving students to the over-fifties, all raring to go!

And go they did! The second the lights went down every night, the tension would begin to rise and the audience would stamp their feet and chant "WE WANT STEPS" at the top of their voices.

And boy, did they get what they asked for! Every night in front of mad-for-it audiences holding up banners declaring their love for the band, Lisa, Lee, H, Claire and Faye performed seventeen mind-blowing songs, including a fantastic

Steps In Private

three-track medley. Incredible dance routines, tons of surprises and loads of audience participation made for a rocking show! Every song was a winner, from the gorgeous ballads to the uplifting favourites to the fantastic disco numbers and the stunning new self-penned songs.

Steps came, they sang, they danced and they flew. Every night the atmosphere was electric and the crowds were stunned with every new twist and turn! Steps entertained people like they'd never been entertained before, and left them desperate for more. There's never been a show quite like it.

If you missed it, you're mad! And if you did see it, you're in good company, because even royalty went along to see the show at Wembley! Princesses Eugenie and Beatrice went to catch the Steppers, as did All Saints, Boyzone, B*Witched, Westlife, a1, Vic Reeves and the Sultan of Brunei, to name but a few. It seems no one can resist a show this good!

Fan-tastic!

Not only did Steps love every minute of performing, but they were really pleased that they had the chance to see loads of their fans while they were on tour.

"The tour is a time when we get to meet lots of the fans because we do meet and greets,"

It's Showtime!

says Lee. "We also get to go out and about and see the fans and say hello. A lot of people get the chance to talk to us about the shows and tell us what they thought.

"It's brilliant because it gives us that chance to say thank you to them for everything."

Some fans will go to great lengths to see the band, as Lisa explains. "Sometimes if fans know where we're staying they check into the same hotels as us, but to be honest it's not a good time to see us. When we're in the hotel we just want to chill out, have a drink and go to bed. We'd much rather see them when we're awake and alert!"

"That's true," says H. "We're getting to spend lots of time seeing them, which is amazing. But we'd much rather see them when we can talk to them properly. For instance, one night I got woken up at three in the morning by some fans, but I was so tired I couldn't even speak to them. I haven't got a clue how they got through to my room because we all go under pseudonyms. It's very odd!"

"We're happy to talk to anyone," says Claire. "But there are times when we need a bit of time to ourselves, like when we're trying to sleep. But most of the fans are really respectful and they know that if we can, we'll go and chat to them."

Steps In Private

So what kind of presents have they been given on the tour? "Oh loads!" smiles Faye, "We've had posters, cards, teddies, the lot. H got really spoilt on his birthday which he loved, and Lisa got a lovely surprise the other day."

"Oh yeah, I got given a lovely little teddy bear!" she beams. "It was really nice because I'd left my Baby Dill at home the day before and I was so upset. I also got given some beautiful flowers, but I can't sleep with them in my room because they get on my chest a bit. So when this lovely girl gave me the teddy I gave her my flowers so I knew they were going to a good home!"

6 Faye In Private

Faye's hotel pseudonym:
Louise Burr. "It's actually one of my best friends' names. She came to visit me once and tried to book in under her name and they wouldn't let her, so she had to go under a pseudonym as well!"

Up Close and Personal with Faye

Faye looks after the rest of the gang on tour. She loves meeting new people on tour and always has a huge smile for everyone she meets. She also loves the odd bit of partying, and her nights out with pals mean that she doesn't suffer too much when it comes to missing home. "I did a lot of travelling before the band so I'm used to being away from home and I don't miss it too much. But I do miss my family and friends quite a lot, especially my mum and dad. Luckily I get to see my sister a lot because she comes to visit me all the time. My friends are brilliant as well,

Steps In Private

they make a real effort to come and see me and I probably get to see them more when I'm on tour than I would usually! We get the chance to go out after the shows and make a night of it, whereas we don't always have that much time when I'm back in London."

When it comes to relaxing. Faye hasn't been able to go swimming on tour because of her hair extensions, but she's found plenty of other ways to unwind. "I'm a bit gutted that I can't go swimming because I love it, it's one of my favourite ways to chill out. But I go shopping a lot instead! I've always been a good shopper and being on tour gives me the chance to shop in loads of different places, which is always nice. Shopping is cool because not only can you get lots of lovely new things but it gets you away from everything. And I do find spending money very therapeutic indeed!"

Unlike most of the band, Faye isn't a huge fan of the gym, and reckons that she's found a much more fun way to get fit! "I like to get my exercise by going to a club and having a good old boogie. It's a much more enjoyable way to get fit. I've never been much of a gym goer so dancing is my substitute."

Faye is also a fan of meditation which helps her to stay balanced and calm.

"I went for Reiki healing some time ago and I

Faye In Private

really enjoyed it. I had a really amazing experience. I was totally hooked from then on and I got really interested in different relaxation techniques.

Then Lisa bought me a meditating kit for Christmas which I loved and I learnt how to do it properly, so now I meditate as often as I need to. If I've had a really good day and I'm quite cheery and awake I'll be fine. But if I've had a really stressful day and I just can't wind down then I'll meditate for about half an hour to an hour and get myself balanced again. It really works."

Faye also clears her head by having a bit of time to herself. "I'll sit in my hotel room or the dressing room on my own and read or watch TV. I like watching TV really late snuggled up in bed when there are tacky chat shows on! I actually need to spend quite a lot of time on my own but I don't really get a chance to that often, so if I can nip off and hide for a while I will. I love to be surrounded by people, and of course we are all the time in this job, but I also like my own company and I need to be on my own sometimes. It's important to get a good balance."

Step back in time!

Being in Steps has been a crazy rollercoaster ride, but the fun is only just beginning for the glit-

Steps In Private

tery fivesome. Faye reflects on her life in Steps so far...

How do you think you've changed since the beginning of Steps?
I don't think I'm as noisy as I was, and I don't think I'm quite as excitable. I think I'm more aware of things, and because we work so hard I constantly keep my eyes open so I can pay attention to what's going on. I think I'm still as ambitious as I was before, and there's still so much I want to do. My friends are still the same friends that I've had for years and years. I really found out who my friends were a long time ago. I don't think any of the band have really changed or got bigheaded at all to be honest, and I think that's because we don't all sit back and look at what we've done and think "Aren't we great!" That's just not our way at all. I think we keep each other down-to-earth.

Did you ever expect the band to come this far?
No, I don't think any of us could have predicted what was going to happen. I think we all got the job and thought "Let's see how it goes," but we really didn't know what to expect at all. We were all open-minded and even now we're still waiting to see where things go. It was a massive buzz when we got our record deal so quickly, and

Faye In Private

from then on everything happened so fast that we didn't have a chance to stop to think about things and realise what was going on around us. So it's still exciting every time something new happens.

What have been the best times for you so far?
I think the BRIT award was our biggest triumph as a band, it meant so much to us. When we were standing on the stage collecting the award we were all looking at each other and smiling and it felt so good. But while awards and record sales are incredible, I also think that some of the best times we've had have been when we're together as a group and we just laugh and laugh.

Is being in the band still as much fun as it always was?
Absolutely! Even now we can still be in fits of giggles about nothing and have the best days ever. When you walk away from those days you realise just how brilliant being in a band like this is.

How have you got through the hard times?
We all support each other and we're always there for each other. It's hard being in the pop

Steps In Private

world because you can get criticised a lot, and we've been heartbroken over some of the things that have been said about us along the way. There have been good days and bad days, it kind of goes in waves, but nothing's ever been so bad that we've felt like giving up or anything. The group means too much to us for that. We've always believed in us as a band and we've always stuck together and I think that has got us through, and always will. We're all still having a really good time after all this time and I'm really happy for us all.

What would people be surprised to discover about you after all this time?

Probably that I'm not as confident as everyone thinks, although I am working on that. People see me on TV and stuff and they think that I'm the most confident person in the world, but I have my moments of insecurity like everyone else. People may also be surprised to hear that I am not leaving Steps, despite what the papers say!

[Another big secret is Faye's tattoo! She has a scorpion in the small of her back which she got in L.A. at the same time as Lee got his.] It really hurt but I was determined to have one. Lee and I were lying there looking at each other and grimacing in pain, but it did

Faye In Private

get a bit less painful after a while. I'd wanted one for ages and I think it really helped having Lee there for support. We kind of spurred each other on!

What's the weirdest rumour you've ever heard about yourself to date?
That I'm going out with a Dutch magician! I was apparently his assistant which is how we met. How ridiculous! It was all over the papers and it's *soooooo* not true. Sometimes I read things about myself and they're so far off the mark, I really don't know where they get them from.

How do you see the future of Steps?
I don't think any of us can really predict what will happen. We've had a new lease of life because we're writing the third album and that's spurred us on to do even more. Now we want to write another album, and then another one after that, and then . . . it might last forever! We'll be there doing "5,6,7,8" when we're eighty!

I Know Him (and Her) so Well!
The other Steppers reveal how their relationship with Faye has changed since the band first started out!

Steps In Private

Claire on Faye
Faye and I have always been close and we know that we can totally count on each other. I don't think I could have got through everything without her and Lisa and the boys. There's a really big connection between me and Faye and we got to know each other really well from the word go. There are times when I'll say to her, "You know what Faye? I really love you!" and she'll say the same to me. There's never been a problem between me and Faye. She always used to come and stay at my house in the beginning, and she's good friends with my mum as well which is so nice. It's a brilliant friendship.

Lisa on Faye
Me and Faye have always got on brilliantly because she's a bit like myself, she's a bit of a party animal and a bit wild. We've always had a brilliant time together. We've always had a very constant friendship and she always knows the right thing to say if you're worrying about something. I suppose that with Claire our friendship was more of a gradual thing, but me and Faye clicked straight away because we bonded through our partying ways!

Lee on Faye
Faye and I clicked right at the beginning at the auditions before we'd even got into the band.

Faye In Private

We started chatting and she was telling me all about what she was doing at the time and it just so happened that we both got picked for Steps. She's a real party animal and I've looked after her when she's been hassled by guys or she's not feeling great, and she always looks after me and sticks up for me. Me and Faye have never really rowed so in that way our relationship hasn't changed. She can tell me to shut up and I can tell her to shut up and it won't mean anything. We're up front with each other and there's a lot of respect there.

H on Faye

The first time I saw Faye I thought she was absolutely stunning. I still remember to this day that she was standing there with her naturally curly hair and these copper trousers on and she totally stood out in the room. She was this tall, leggy blonde and she was just perfect for the band. Faye was always really up for clubbing and at that time I'd be going out and partying every night so we'd both go out a lot. But now our workload is so huge that I can't go out every night and still get up the next morning! But I know that if I want a good night out Faye will still be up for it. She's a brilliant laugh and she's always the last one in the bar and the last one to bed. In that way she hasn't changed a bit!

Steps In Private

Lisa's lonely hearts ad for Faye
"Bubbly blonde seeks a funky male who shares a love of glitter to share crazy nights out!" Anyone who has a night out with Faye will have a crazy night!

7 Step On It!

As the Steps tour is such a huge affair, the fivesome wanted to make sure that they were as comfortable as possible when they made their long journeys from venue to venue.

So tour buses – which can be pretty noisy and squashed – went out the window, and in came super-luxurious Galaxy Space Cruisers. Each vehicle can hold up to eight people and, as Steps had three between them, they had plenty of space to kick back and relax. And, of course, sleep after too much partying!

The initial idea was for one van to carry all the luggage and the other two to accommodate the band – but things didn't quite work out that way! Due to the fact that it was H's birthday during the tour and all of the band members were doing rather a lot of shopping, the luggage had to be shared out between all three vans!

"We have got loads and loads of bags. We've got so much luggage you wouldn't believe it,"

Steps In Private

admits H. "But thankfully this tour is a lot easier than the last one because we spend three or four days in each town so, we don't have to unpack our cases every day."

Their tour manager John, and their bodyguards Brett and Sel, drive the gang around, and there are no hard and fast rules when it comes to sharing. "It's just whoever gets to the vans first and hops in." Lisa explains. "It changes every day. Everyone jumps in with different people, it keeps things interesting!"

H has been a particularly popular travelling companion due to his fantastic massage mat which hangs over a chair in one of the vans. "It's amazing," says a wide-eyed H. "I've got it over my seat and I have it on while travelling to relax me. You plug it into the cigarette lighter in the car and it's like having someone massaging you for hours. It does a pulsing massage, or a shiatsu massage, or a kneading massage. It's perfect for when I've been on stage and I'm a bit achy. I couldn't be without it now."

Needless to say, the rest of the band were desperate to have a go when they spotted it. But while they all agree that it feels fantastic, they're not so keen on its other functions. "It plays these sounds," Faye explains warily. "You can have birds tweeting, or the sound of water flowing, and they're both really annoying. The

Step On It!

birds get irritating after about two minutes, and the water sounds like someone's going to the loo. It makes you feel like you need to go all the time which is a nightmare when you're driving for hours at a time!"

Lee also finds the sounds a bit unnerving when he's travelling with H. "I've had H sitting behind me quite a lot, and he makes all these funny noises when he's got his massage seat switched on. We'll be going down the motorway at eighty miles an hour and all you can hear are birds tweeting behind you and H moaning and groaning. It's very odd."

But that hasn't stopped Lee. "I was the first one to try it out," he says proudly. "H brought it to my hotel room on the first day of the tour and plugged it in and was going "Go on, go on! Have a go!" He really thought it was the best thing ever, but I was just staring at it thinking he'd gone mad. It wasn't until I tried it out that I realised how fantastic it is. It's so relaxing."

The dancers travel separately to the band on a huge, swanky, gold tour bus which boasts bunk beds and even a kitchen! "I sampled the delights of the dancers' tour bus a couple of times," laughs Lisa. "I fancied a change so I hitched a ride with them and watched a video. It's got a Playstation and a TV at one end, and a

Steps In Private

kitchen area at the other. It was really good fun!"

So how do the guys and gals while away the hours travelling between venues? Chatterbox Claire is constantly on the phone to her family and her friends back home.

"My phone bills are outrageous, but there's nothing better than having a good gossip to pass the time!"

And it's possible that Claire's phone bills are about to get worse. She's just got a very swish Internet mobile phone, which means that she'll be able to surf the net on the move. "I'm going to have to be really careful otherwise. I'll spend a fortune," she says sounding worried. Claire's also been listening to loads of music on the move, in particular Backstreet Boys, Deborah Cox, 'N Sync and Destiny's Child.

Lisa loves a bit of music while she's travelling the country as well, and her current favourites are the most recent albums by Jordan Knight, Whitney Houston and Britney Spears.

"I've also been listening to a bit of garage here and there, but it's not very relaxing!" she says.

Lisa also passes the time by reading and playing on her Gameboy. "We all take our Gameboys with us everywhere. I couldn't be without mine now," she says.

Lee's also a real Gameboy guy, and he's also

Step On It!

discovered a fab new game on his friend's mobile phone that he's become addicted to. "It's this square and you have to kind of turn all these numbers around and rearrange them so that all the numbers are in the right order," he explains cryptically. "I know it sounds a bit weird, but it's really good fun and I've wasted hours doing it. I haven't got it on my phone but Faye's got it on hers, and my mate Dave has it on his so I keep nicking their phones every five minutes." And talking of phones, Lee's been spending rather a lot of time on his! "Well that's what it's for! But I'm not as bad as Claire, no way . . ."

Faye stops herself getting bored by reading loads of magazines, listening to music, playing her Gameboy and getting onto her mobile and calling everyone! "It's going to be a close call between me and Claire as to who'll have the biggest phone bill after this tour. We're terrible," says Faye. "But thankfully my Muppets game on my Gameboy has kept me amused and away from my phone quite a lot!"

As well as chilling out on his massage mat, H has been reading loads of books. Or rather, listening to them!

"I'm a bit lazy when it comes to reading so I've bought a load of talking books instead," he confides. "I really can't be bothered to read, isn't that terrible?!

Steps In Private

"Anyone who wants to swot up on their English at school should buy a talking book. Funnily enough I've actually bought a book that I was supposed to read in school and never did. It's *Animal Farm* by George Orwell. I haven't read it yet, though. Well, listened to it I should say . . . I've been listening to quite a lot of autobiographies because generally the writers will read the books.

"I read Fergie's and when Princesses Eugenie and Beatrice came to see the show we met them afterwards and I said, 'Tell your mum I read her book!' It was really good."

H also curbed his boredom by sending rude text messages to the rest of the band on his mobile. "Some of them were really naughty poems and stuff. We were too shocked to message him back!" Claire laughs.

Hold On, Isn't That ...

How would you react if you walked into a restaurant and saw your favourite pop band sitting having a meal? Well that's what's been happening to loads of people as Steps travel around the country. They've been stopping off at garages and service stations from Glasgow to Wales to grab themselves some food and stock up on drinks and magazines. So how do people react

Step On It!

when they see Britain's biggest and best pop band walk in while they're having a spot of dinner?

"When we walk into a restaurant and we're all together it's a real shock to people," Claire says. "Obviously they don't expect us to be there so they stop and stare. I can't blame them, I'd do the same!"

Lisa reckons that people react in different ways. "Some people will come straight over and ask for our autographs, but others will just sit there whispering and looking at us for ages. It's so funny."

"The funniest thing is when we stop off at a garage and we pop in to get a drink or whatever," says Faye. "You can see people looking at you and wondering if it's you or not because they don't expect a band to be at a petrol station in the middle of nowhere. I think I'm particularly conspicuous because of my hair. Dreadlocks are not the best disguise!"

Claire, however, says that she doesn't always get recognised. "I just put a cap and sunglasses on and I'm fine. I really don't get recognised that much," she says. Well, now you know what to look out for!

Despite them being five of the most recognisable faces in Britain, there are even times when people don't recognise any of the band! As

Steps In Private

H explains, "We were travelling from Glasgow to Newcastle and we went to a burger bar in the middle of nowhere and I don't think anyone recognised us because they didn't expect us to be there. I think if anyone had said that we'd just been in there they wouldn't have believed it anyway. We didn't even get asked for our autograph. We just sat and ate our food quietly!"

But because not being recognised is such a rare occurrence in Steps World, the band have three bodyguards with them at all times who are on hand to escort them whenever they want to go out. Since fame has kicked in in a huge way the band find it hard to go anywhere without being noticed. And while the Steppers are always more than happy to sign autographs and pose for pictures, there are times when things can get a little out of hand and groups of fans have literally tried to rip the band's clothes off just so that they have some kind of memento of their meeting.

"It can get pretty scary at times," says H. "We have had people grabbing onto our clothes, and even our hair!"

"But thankfully most of the time our fans are really lovely," says Lee. "I think we've got some of the politest fans in pop!"

8 H In Private

H's hotel pseudonym:
Mr. G. String. "We were just thinking up stupid names one day and I came up with that. I've also used Mr. A. Capella before as well. We have to change them all the time though because our fans are too clever!"

Up Close and Personal with H
H is the most cheerful fella imaginable both on tour and off. He loves travelling around the country performing to thousands of people and meeting the fans, but as he explains, he does hanker after home sometimes. "I definitely get homesick quite a lot and I start to really miss my friends and family. But I take pictures of them with me and put them all around me in my hotel room so that I can see them all the time! I keep in touch with all my friends and family by phone as well, although I don't have as much time to call them as I used to because I'm usually asleep

Steps In Private

when we're travelling! But at least my phone bills aren't too bad, they're not sky high like some people I could mention!

There's no doubt that H lives up to his Hyperactive nickname, so he definitely needs time to relax sometimes! He's been into meditation for some time, and has recently become a big fan of yoga. "I still meditate when I need to and I find that it really helps me, but yoga is also a brilliant way to chill out. It's quite hard and it takes you a while to get into it because of the positions and stuff, but I'm getting more used to it. I've just put a gym into my house and I've got my yoga mat and stuff in there, and I've got a CD player so I can play some nice music while I'm twisting myself around!"

So how did this love of yoga come about? "I got into it after the last tour because things were really hectic. I'd got very used to meditating so I needed something else to channel my energies into. I'm not brilliant at it, but I'm going to learn. People think that yoga is for girls but it's actually really hard work. Faye said once that she wanted to do yoga and the guy that taught Geri Halliwell sent his number over to her, so I need to get his number and start learning with him."

There's no doubt that H is a people person and he's always at the centre of everything, but

H In Private

even the most sociable person in pop needs some chilling out time on his own. "I've been getting up early and going to the gym. It's such a good way to start the day and it makes you feel so much better. And the good thing about going down there early is that there's no one else around so I get time to myself. I've even been beating Lee in there most mornings, which is amazing. But I made a pact with myself to go as often as possible and I'm doing really well so far. I'll have a six-pack before you know it!" H laughs, "Then I'm gonna strip off and show everyone!" Keep your eyes open, H fans!

Step Back in Time!

It's been a crazy rollercoaster ride, but it's only just beginning for the glittery fivesome. H reflects on his life in Steps so far . . .

How do you think you've changed since the beginning of Steps?

I don't think I have changed that much. I think we're all pretty grounded people and even though things are going mad around us I take it with a pinch of salt and think "I'm a very lucky person, I can't believe this is all happening to me." I think as long as we think of it in that respect and keep it all in perspective

Steps In Private

we'll be fine, we won't change at all. I've learned a lot over the past few years so I suppose I'm different in that way. And I've also learned to trust all the people around me and to trust my friends. I don't think I've calmed down though. I've always been the same and I always will be!

Did you ever expect the band to come this far?
I always hoped, but I've never actually sat down and thought about how well we've done because we're constantly on the go. I appreciate everything that we've gone through and everything we've achieved. I was always very optimistic when we first started and I thought "5,6,7,8" was going to be number one everywhere. It was in a lot of countries but not in the UK, but I always felt really positive. When people knock you down it makes you want to do even better, and luckily for us we used people's insults or negative comments and channelled them and did even better. Now we've got the last laugh. People laughed when we released a line-dancing track, and they laughed when we released an album, then they laughed when we did a tour, now we're laughing even louder! As long as we're having a laugh, who cares what other people say?

H In Private

Is being in the band still as much fun as it always was?
Oh yes, we try to have as much fun as we can. Obviously the workload is still quite heavy. People think that when you become successful the workload eases off, but you actually have to work harder to maintain the success you've got. But we do still all get on with each other really well, and we're always laughing. You've got to let your hair down and go wild every now and again!

What have been the best times for you so far?
There have been so many brilliant achievements and we've done so many things that we wanted to do. For me one of the best things was when Claire and I presented *Steps To The Stars*. Presenting is something that I'd love to do more of in the future. Of course we all loved winning the BRIT award, and we all had the time of our lives at the album launch for *Steptacular*. And of course flying on the tour is amazing because it's something that I've always wanted to do. There's still so much more I want to do though. One of my dreams is to go on stage in a musical in the West End, that's definitely another move for me.

How have you got through the hard times?
We're all there for each other because we're all going through the same things. As I said,

Steps In Private

we turn negative things into positives and carry on and become even more determined. I think that's always been our attitude and it's got us through everything. The hard times really pale into insignificance when you have so many brilliant things happening to you all the time. We try to concentrate on the good stuff.

What would people be surprised to discover about you after all this time?
I guess that what you see with me is what you get. You take me as you find me, it's not a front, I really am like I am. This is meeeeeee!

What's the weirdest rumour that you've heard about yourself to date?
That me and Lisa were going out. It's been around for years now but it's never been true. There's nothing whatsoever going on there, but people still bring it up all the time! There was also all the stuff in the papers about us boys earning more than the girls. It was so stupid, it must have been a quiet day for the papers and someone just decided to make it up. There were debate programmes about it and everything, people were using it as an example of inequality to women and getting really irate and it wasn't

H In Private

even true. There's no way the girls would let us get away with that!

How do you see the future of Steps?
We take each day as it comes now. There's still a lot that we want to do. We're going to America, and we're doing a lot of songwriting now. I think we'd all like to try some solo stuff at some point later on as well. We'll obviously be staying within the band, but trying some things on our own to see how we get on. Other bands have released solo singles and stayed together, it's just like a natural progression really. We all work really well together, but I think it's a case of proving to ourselves and to the public that we can do it. I'd love to do a duet with Britney Spears, that would be brilliant.

I Know Him (and Her) so Well!
The other Steppers reveal how their relationship with H has changed since the group first started out!

Claire on H
What can I say about H? We hit it off from the start because we were both the youngest. And while I'm not as hyperactive as him, I think we

Steps In Private

have the same kind of mentality. We always have a laugh and we can talk to each other about things, and he'll always be really honest with me. He can be a bit tactless at times, but that's just H, he's a nutter! We both love singing, which was a big bonding thing for us, and we were both the untrained band members so we used to understand the way the other one was feeling when we were learning new dance routines. We could sympathise with each other!

Faye on H

Me and H have got a funny relationship. I'm quite serious compared to him, and he's up and bouncy all the time, he just never stops, but I wouldn't change him for the world. We've had some great nights out together and he's even been known to be a good listener! He's very confident and sometimes I wish I could do the things he does. He'll always be the one that will get us all laughing if anything is going wrong and you can always count on him to cheer up a situation.

Lisa on H

H is brilliant and we bonded from day one because we're both Welsh. We're the wacky Welsh and we had a mad friendship from the

H In Private

first time we met! We just have such a laugh, really good fun. We're very naughty and we giggle a lot and sometimes I laugh until I cry when I'm in his company. I'm sure we drive everyone up the wall sometimes because we just don't stop, especially when people are trying to be all serious or trying to do an interview with us. He's brilliant!

Lee on H
H is as wacky as ever! I think I still get on exactly the same with H as I have from day one. I think we're a bit closer than the rest because we're both guys and we share dressing rooms on the tour and stuff. H is great because he does his own thing and he's so hyper. Some people love him for that and maybe some people don't but the brilliant thing about H is that he doesn't care what other people think. Sometimes I wish I had that attitude because he does what he wants to do and he gets on with it regardless. I think that's brilliant. If he's being too loud at the wrong moment I'll give him a certain look and sometimes he'll shut up. Then again sometimes he'll just carry on, it depends how mischievous he's feeling. But I think that maybe he listens to me more than he does to the girls. It's a boy thing – and I'm bigger than him!

Steps In Private

Claire's lonely hearts ad for H
"Hyperactive, energetic blue-eyed blonde bombshell seeks fun-loving, outgoing nutcase!"

9 Tragedy! It's Time For Work

Ever wondered what happens on a swish Steps photo shoot? Well now you can find out as we take you for a sneaky peak behind the scenes!

Music website Worldpop.com sponsored the entire Steps tour. And one afternoon Steps and the Worldpop.com team decided to get together to create some gorgeous pictures that could be used for promotion and displayed in all their glory on the website. The shoot took place in a huge swanky room in a hotel in Newcastle, and there were around twenty people on hand making sure that the shoot ran smoothly!

The Steppers have hired a huge hotel suite to get ready in, but before they go about beautifying themselves, they set about ordering lunch as they're all starving! H gets on the phone to room service and orders the chow while the others busy themselves deciding what to wear. "Can I just enquire about some

Steps In Private

food please?" H says in his poshest voice. "Yes, I'll have some vegetables on lentils and some mashed potato . . ." he continues, while the others shout their requests to him.

While they're waiting for the food to arrive they all have their hair and make-up done to make sure that they're glamorous and shine-free when the photographer begins snapping! Steps' lovely make-up artist Jackie, who works with the band constantly, has travelled up from London, along with Kenny their swish stylist who has brought loads of beautiful clothes for them to try on and choose from.

As Faye did her own make-up before she arrived she settles down to watch TV and paint her nails with her new shimmery MAC nail varnish. Everyone is really chuffed when they realise that Supermarket Sweep is on. "Ooh, I love this, and that means that Jerry Springer's on next," Lisa says excitedly. Lee and H have a look through the clothes and try to decide on an outfit. Faye checks the togs out while Lisa joins her to peruse the accessories! Lisa is very excited by the fine array of sparkly jewellery that's on offer and she coos with delight as she tries on various shimmery numbers.

H tries on a silver bracelet and immediately lets out a howl. "It pinched my wrist!" he cries. Instead of offering sympathy everyone laughs

Tragedy! It's Time For Work

hysterically while he writhes in pain and tries to pull it off. The more he's trying to unclasp it, the tighter it's getting and he has to get Kenny to help him. "Owwww, my wrist's killing me!" he complains when Kenny eventually gets it off. Next he tries on some big Elvis-style shades and starts swaggering around the room. "I look like my father!" he laughs checking out his reflection in the bathroom mirror. "Nah, you look more like Elvis!" Lisa smiles as the others roll their eyes and chuckle.

With their make-up done, Claire and Lisa set about selecting their outfits and nip in and out of the bathroom to get dressed. The band passed the point of being embarrassed about getting changed in front of each other a long time ago, but there are people in the room that they don't know very well.

"We don't even think about stripping off in front of each other any more, it's second nature because we've done it so many times," Lisa says. "But I think people might be a bit shocked if we start doing it in front of them. They'll think we're real exhibitionists!"

After choosing their clothes, Claire and Lisa get back on the accessories trail, and Claire falls in love with a pair of yellow-tinted sunglasses that are decorated with a little diamante heart. "They're so gorgeous, and

Steps In Private

because they've got a tint I could wear them at night as well," Claire says showing them off to the rest of the band. Needless to say by the end of the shoot she's decided that she's going to buy them, and Kenny arranges for her to take them there and then.

"Claire's amazing," Lee says shaking his head, "she can shop anywhere!"

By the time the food eventually arrives everyone's starving. The waitress knocks on the door and H runs over to let her in. His face lights up when he spots his lunch. "I love you!" he tells her, and she looks like she's going to explode with delight.

They all tuck in straight away. "Eurgh, yours looks like rabbit droppings!" Lisa laughs, eyeing H's food.

"Actually they're lentils, and they're very good for you," he says adopting his posh voice once again. H offers everyone some of his mashed potato. "Who will *buuuuuy* my mashed potato?" he sings at the top of his voice, mimicking a song from the classic musical *Oliver!*.

"He does this all the time," Lisa explains rolling her eyes, "If we're stuck in traffic he opens the door and sings at the top of his voice. He did it to this woman who was getting married the other day. Luckily she thought it was really funny."

Tragedy! It's Time For Work

Once all the food has been devoured (except H's rabbit droppings, which remain in a pile on his plate) the shoot begins. The girls are up first and they pout to perfection.

They're all experts in the art of posing, having done a zillion photo shoots over the past three years.

Next it's the boys' turn to pucker up and play up for the camera. They try their hardest to look as professional as possible while the girls stand behind the camera taking the mickey out of their poses.

The group shot comes next and the fivesome cuddle up together on a huge, squashy sofa. The first picture is about to be taken when Lisa's mobile goes off. "Oh Liiiiiiisaaaaa!" they all shout.

"I'll have to call you back, we're kind of in the middle of something!" Lisa tells her friend sheepishly. The camera starts clicking and the gang gets into position. They're naturals in front of the camera, holding hands and leaning on each other just like you would if you were cuddling up to your mum.

So what's the secret of their success? How do they still get on so well despite having to spend practically every waking moment together? "We love each other," Claire explains matter-of-factly. "Sometimes we bicker and

Steps In Private

things can get a little bit fraught, but we're such good mates and we know each other so well. You get to know everyone's moods and you automatically know how they're feeling.

"There are so many bands that don't understand each other, but there's a lot of give and take with us. We don't always like each other, but we do genuinely love each other."

The shoot is over and it's time to be interviewed. They're all being interviewed individually on camera. Needless to say when each Stepper takes their place in front of the camera the others take great joy in standing behind the camera pulling faces and trying to put them off. H is the most easily led, and instead of ignoring his fellow band members he keeps getting the giggles and having to restart the interview!

Despite having been interviewed about everything from what colour pants they wear to their philosophy on life, the Steppers always manage to find something new and interesting to say in interviews. "We have so many things happening to us all the time that there's always something different to say," Lee says. "There's always something going on, whether we're visiting different countries or just hanging out together. Nothing is ever straightforward with us!"

Once all the interviews are completed the band are all heading back to the hotel to get

Tragedy! It's Time For Work

ready as they're planning to go out for a Chinese meal later that night. They've got a night off and they plan to make the most of it!

"Come on Mna's!" Lisa shouts to them all, calling them by the band's pet name for each other. "I got the name from my brother Andrew," Lisa explains of the strange moniker. "Whenever he was singing a song and he didn't know the words he'd fill it in by singing "mna, mna, mna". So I started using the word when I was talking to the others. Me and H use it all the time now.

"In fact, H tried to ban it about a year ago because he woke up one morning and couldn't get it out of his head. I wouldn't expect anyone to understand because it means nothing, but it also means so many things to us."

"The cars are waiting outside for us, it's time to go everyone!" Claire shouts to her band pals as they grab their bags and head for the door. They kiss everyone goodbye and politely thank them for all their help on the shoot. Then in a whirlpool of glitter and grins they're gone – off to find the best Chinese restaurant in town!

10 Lisa In Private

Lisa's hotel pseudonym:
Jan Nash. "I go under the name Jan Nash because it was my mum's maiden name."

Up Close and Personal with Lisa

Lovely Lisa is a feisty gal and no mistake! But while she's a glitzy party girl who likes nothing better than a rousing night out, she does miss home when she's out on tour for weeks on end. And while her heart still belongs to Wales, it's London she misses when she's away. "I don't get homesick for my house in Wales any more which is really weird. I get homesick for my house in London. We've got our own places now and I guess you tend to miss what's yours. I really miss my family when I'm away but they travel a lot to see me. They'll come to visit me in London a lot, and Birmingham, Manchester and Wales if we're playing there. They're really committed and I appreciate it hugely.

Lisa In Private

"When I am back in London the brilliant thing is that my brothers are in a band called 3SL and they're travelling down to London twice a week to work on the band, so I'm getting to see them more than ever. It's lovely because I'm really close to them. Another good thing about performing in London is that a lot of my friends can come to see us and check out the show. Also I get to go home to my lovely house and sleep in my own bed which is brilliant because you can get a bit sick of hotels. Then again, the good thing about hotels is that someone's cleaning up after you all the time!"

Lisa's a real people person and is always the life and soul of every party, but even a party girl needs time to herself. So just how does the bonkers redhead chill out? "I like to go for walks on my own so I'll try to sneak out of the hotel and go for a walk, but usually one of the security guards will catch me and they'll end up coming with me! Walking helps me gather my thoughts and I can also get some fresh air. We're stuck in hotels all the time so I like to get out and about whenever I can. I also like going to the gym. I generally go every morning and that really chills me well because it gets out a lot of stress. I'm much more into the gym these days than I used to be. I think Lee's been a good influence on me! It was always a real effort for me

Steps In Private

to actually go, and I used to go just because I thought I should, but now I genuinely enjoy it and I look forward to going. I often see Lee in there as well so it's good to have some company.

"If we get a couple of hours free time I'll go and have a sauna or a massage and totally chill out. There's nothing better than a stress-relieving massage when you've been sitting in a car for hours."

When she needs to get away from everything and everyone on tour Lisa's hotel room beckons and she'll hide herself away and catch a bit of Jerry Springer! "I like to watch TV in my room. I think I definitely need to take time out sometimes. We've got such a heavy schedule and things can be so hectic that you need to keep your feet on the ground. Sometimes you can be surrounded by so many people and you kind of want to be on your own."

And if the band get a bit of time away from the madness of the pop world Lisa will swiftly make her way back to Wales for a bit of clean air and mountain walking! "If we've got a few days off I love to go back home to Wales and go for a walk in the mountains and by the lakes because it's so peaceful. It's so beautiful there. It's somewhere I like to go and be on my own because there's no one around for miles. It's incredible."

Lisa In Private

Step back in time!

It's been a crazy rollercoaster ride, but it's only just beginning for the glittery fivesome. Lisa reflects on her life in Steps so far . . .

How do you think you've changed since the beginning of Steps?

I've learned a lot about the industry, and a lot about the others. I've always been very determined and I was so desperate to be in a band and be famous, and now I'm here I feel like I can relax a bit more and really enjoy it. I've learned that if you really want something you can get it, I really believe that. It's been so worth all the hard work. I'd tell anyone who's sitting in their room singing along to Britney and dreaming of being a pop star that you can do it. Just go for it!

What have been the best times for you so far?

For me having the second album go in at number one was a fantastic achievement. The first album got to number two so it was nice that we had a little room for improvement. It was brilliant to go straight in to number one because we stayed there for weeks and kept a lot of other acts off the top spot. I think we were a bit unpopular with other bands for a while!

Steps In Private

Did you ever expect the band to come this far?
Oh gosh, it's surpassed all my hopes and dreams, it really has. I wanted the world and for us to be as successful as we could and still be happy and still be friends. We've got that and more, and things just keep getting better.

Is being in the band still as much fun as it always was?
Totally! I still laugh as much now as I did when the band first got together. Things may have got a bit more serious business-wise, but we still know how to party!

How have you got through the hard times?
With the help of the others. It was really difficult for me losing my privacy. Obviously fame has been a gradual thing and it's something that I've always wanted so I wouldn't change it for the world. But fame is a one-way road, and once you're on the road there's no going back. Fame has got its fantastic points and its advantages, like you get good tables in restaurants and a box in the theatre, and that's fantastic. But the downside is when I go to the pub. My friends treat me like their mate Lisa, not Lisa from Steps, which is great. But other people that are around just see me as Lisa from Steps, so very

Lisa In Private

often people will come over and ask for my autograph and it kind of shatters my normality. It's difficult when you're trying to have a normal moment and you feel like you can't escape. But as I said, there are so many more positive points to what we do.

What's the weirdest rumour you've ever heard about yourself to date?
It's got to be the one about me and H dating. It's been around for ages now and it's just started up again on our website because H pinched my bum during "Better The Devil You Know" on the tour and thousands of people saw it. Everyone thinks that there's something going on but of course there isn't, he's like a brother to me.

What would people be surprised to learn about you after all this time?
That I can turn on light switches and open doors with my feet. I've got a very high kick! If I'm carrying two cups of tea or two dinners, I can reach my leg up and turn the door handle. It's a sight to behold!

How do you see the future of Steps?
The future's bright! Steps have got a lot to do yet and we still feel like we've only just started. I really do think that we're going to play a part in

Steps In Private

musical history. I think we'll be remembered in many years to come. There are a lot of other bands coming up now, and I think we've inspired a lot of other artists which is incredibly flattering. I feel so proud of what we've achieved but there's plenty more to come!

I Know Him (and Her) so Well!

The other Steppers reveal how their relationship with Lisa has changed since the group first started out!

H on Lisa

Me and Lisa had a laugh from day one. We always see the funny side of everything and we're like brother and sister. In this business it's so intense that you have to have a giggle. Me and Lisa shouldn't be put together when we're doing interviews because we're awful, we just make everybody laugh. You can't get any sense out of us. We're the naughty pair, we're always getting into trouble. I think we'll always be the same!

Claire on Lisa

Me and Lisa weren't really, really good friends for about the first one-and-a-half to two years that the band were together. But when we went

Lisa In Private

to America last year we spent a lot of time together and got to know each other really well. I don't think we could ever really understand each other's lives. She was out partying all the time and I didn't want to do that. But after spending time together we've become really close and we can have real girlie chats and sit and gossip and gossip. She's one of my best friends now. It was just weird the way that after all that time me and Lisa just clicked. It feels really special because I know that I've got a true friend there. I can tell her anything and I trust her with everything. Lisa knows everything about me and she always makes me feel so much better if I'm feeling bad about things. She's a little bit older than me and she's experienced the world, so she always has the best advice.

Faye on Lisa

Lisa's always been a party animal – she's always been my partner in crime! We don't party quite as much as we used to because we've moved houses and we don't live that near to each other any more, but we still go out together whenever we get the chance and hit the town and have the time of our lives. We go out and have a good boogie and we're great gossips! We could gossip forever. You should hear us in the dressing room when the three of us girls are together. It's unbelievable!

Lee on Lisa
Lisa is very strong-willed and strong-minded but we understand each other really well. Lisa's always been the one that's there being my friend if I've had problems with girls or anything. I know that I can still really lean on her and she'll give me sound advice. She's great.

H's lonely hearts ad for Lisa
"Feisty redhead requires Welsh-speaking, intelligent man for nights of passion and spicy takeaways!" Lisa needs someone who loves partying just as much as her!

11 After The Work Is Done...!

Partying is the first things on Steps' minds! Wherever they are, after a hectic show, there's nothing the Steppers like better than chilling out and having a drink in the hotel bar.

They all agree that they're all buzzing so much after doing such an energetic, uplifting show they need to wind down and relax with their dancers and any friends and family that have come to visit. "Most of us like to party, especially after a show because you're on such a high," says party girl Lisa. "You've pulled off a great show and you've all done it together, so you want to have a winding-down period. We all stayed up until about four o'clock on the first night in Glasgow because we were celebrating and we were given some champagne to say congratulations. We were all so excited that we'd got through the first night and it had all run smoothly, there's no way we could have gone straight to bed!"

Steps In Private

Faye agrees. "The first night is always the best night because everyone's overexcited and you get such a buzz out of the performance that you just have to party and go a bit mad! And let's just say we did . . . There were some fans in the hotel so we were chatting to them and finding out what they thought of the show. It made us feel even happier when they told how much they loved it, so we celebrated some more!"

If you're thinking that Lisa and Faye sound like the biggest partiers, you'd be right. As Faye says, "We've definitely been labelled as the party animals. We've been trying to quash those rumours and not be the last one to bed every night, but we haven't done terribly well. I think we're all pretty good at partying though. We've all had some real stonking late nights."

"I'd have to say me and Faye are the most rock'n'roll out of all of us though," Lisa admits. "Although Claire's been getting worse lately and staying up later. Then again, Faye and I would say that she's actually getting better because that's a good thing!"

"That's true," Claire chips in. "I've been out quite a few times and had some really late nights. But it's not very clever because I'm a bit hoarse at the moment. I'm going to have to go to bed early with some cocoa from now on! Ahem."

After The Work Is Done ...!

So how good are the boys at partying? "H isn't very rock'n'roll, he's more pop'n'soul!" giggles Lisa.

"Yep," H grins. "I try to be a wild rock'n'roll animal but I always end up getting tired and going to bed! I'll leave the real partying to the girls."

Lee agrees with H, and often favours staying in his room playing Playstation, in particular a game called Syphon Filter 2, over hitting the town or hanging out in the bar. "I know it's not very rock'n'roll but it helps me to chill out. Especially if I'm playing against someone and I beat them, then I can go to bed happy! I do go down to the bar and chill with everyone some nights, but I also like to have a bit of time to myself so I make sure I get a good balance."

But while Lee and H are happy to have more subdued nights, it seems like the girls find it pretty impossible to stay in their rooms and have a quiet evening in.

They'd much rather be in the thick of things, and have even been known to go down to the bar in their pyjamas!

As Claire explains, "It's hard when you come off stage to go straight to bed because your adrenalin is pumping. I just can't sleep. The other day I tried to go straight to bed and I ended up getting up and going downstairs in my

Steps In Private

pyjamas to see everyone. I think it was the fact that I knew everyone would be having a good time and I wanted to be with them chatting about the show and having a laugh. I know we spend all our time together, but I miss the rest of the band when I'm on my own!"

Lisa has also been known to don her PJ's and go in search of a party. "Well why not?" she laughs. "That way you can have a good time, and then when you're ready to sleep you can go straight up to your room and get into bed. Perfect!"

All of the band reckon that it's the family atmosphere on the tour that makes the bar such a fun place to hang out. "Everyone is friends with everyone," explains Faye, "We make a point of getting to know our crew, the people that work on the set or do our lovely catering, so that they all come out for a drink and have a good time. We want everyone to enjoy the Steps tour!"

And judging by the amount of time the crew spend hanging out in the bar, they're certainly doing that!

H's Double Birthday Celebration!

Party part one!
H celebrated his 24th birthday during the tour – twice! The lucky fella got to have two

After The Work Is Done...!

rocking nights out, one in Glasgow and one in London. The rest of the band kicked off the celebrations during a show in Glasgow, when they got the audience to sing "Happy Birthday" to H.

"I got a bit tearful actually," H admits. "Having that many people singing to you is totally overwhelming."

After the show the band, crew and dancers went for a meal before hitting a casino! H fills us in on the fun, "We had a free dinner put on for us in our hotel, which was fantastic. It was Indian food and it was amazing. In fact, Lisa says that its the best Indian food she's ever had. I got lots of pressies and cards and I felt thoroughly spoilt.

"Then afterwards we went to a casino, which was fantastic because it's the first time I've ever been. I didn't gamble at all, I just really enjoyed watching. It was really exciting and we all got dolled up. We looked like something out of the Abba video for "Money, Money, Money", we were all glitzy and glamorous! But I have to admit I was so tired after all the excitement that I was one of the first to bed and I went at about two. Some of the other members of the band didn't get to bed until about five. Thank goodness we didn't have to work the next day!"

Steps In Private

Party part two!

H's second bash was held in the backstage bar at Wembley Arena, where all his friends and family arranged a night to remember! "Everyone had to come as 80s pop stars, and for some reason most people came as Adam Ant!" H laughs. "Unfortunately I also went as Adam Ant, but I was lucky and I got to go to the BBC costume department so I cheated. My costume was really good, but the only problem was that my trousers split about halfway through the evening so I spent the whole night showing my pants to everyone!"

But even that little hitch didn't spoil H's fun.

"It was just perfect. We had George Michael and Madonna lookalikes serving drinks, a Club Tropicana-style bar, and Hawaiian flowers hanging up all over the room.

"The only music that was played was fantastically cheesy 80s stuff, and everyone was up dancing having a massive laugh."

Was the party a complete surprise to H? "Not completely. I kind of knew what they were doing because they told me that the party was going to have an 80s theme, but I didn't expect it to be so brilliant. They worked really hard on it and I was really touched. All my friends and family travelled from Wales to come, and of course the band and all the support acts came along

After The Work Is Done ...!

so it was a really special night. I got given so many presents from everyone. But even though like everyone else I love getting presents, what meant more was getting to spend time with my family and my mates because we haven't all been together for a while."

And you'll be glad to hear that H was the last one up for his second birthday bash! "Yes, I'm proud to say that me and my family and friends were the last ones in the bar. We were being really loud and singing Welsh songs at the top of our voices. All the people working there must have thought we were mad!"

No change there, then!

WESTLIFE: IN REAL LIFE
THE OFFICIAL BOOK

Lise Hand

Straightforward biographies are fine for a group just making their mark in the pop world. But Westlife are different, and this official book is far more than a straightforward biography. With a record-breaking run of singles debuting at number one, and five great personalities, Westlife have a remarkable story to tell, and that story is told in full in *Westlife: In Real Life*.

Author Lise Hand has spent time on the road with Westlife, and through in-depth interviews with Bryan, Nicky, Mark, Shane and Kian gives a real insight into the Westlife world.

Backstage photographs illustrating Westlife's amazing career so far show us what real life is like for the guys as they travel from show to show, giving interviews and press calls, trying to catch some sleep where they can, but loving every minute of the lifestyle they've always wanted.

This feature-packed book answers the questions every Westlife fan wants to ask: What do they think of the hotels they stay in? What's the first thing they do in new cities - explore, shop, sleep or go clubbing? What happens backstage at their shows? Do the boys get homesick? What does a tour manager do?

With exclusive photos, including some taken by the guys themselves in their free time, plus first-hand new interviews and some stunning studio snaps, this is the book no Westlife fan can afford to be without.

ISBN 1 85227 995 8 (hardback)
ISBN 0 7535 0588 6 (paperback)

£14.99/£4.99

BRITNEY SPEARS – THE ILLUSTRATED STORY
THE UNOFFICIAL BOOK

Amanda Stevens

Young, talented and beautiful, teen superstar Britney Spears is the pop artist everyone's talking about. Her sassy, upbeat tunes, including '...Baby One More Time' and 'Oops! ...I Did It Again' have hit the number one spot, while her albums have sold in excess of 20 million copies worldwide.

As well as her international chart success, Britney is one of the world's most talked about celebrities, with newspapers and magazines reporting her every move and eagerly anticipating her new album.

Full to the brim with great photos and fascinating facts, this unofficial book tells the full story of Britney's incredible journey from talented tot to international megastar, with features on her amazing videos, irresistible music and superstar style. It's a must for every Britney fan!

ISBN 07535 0592 4

£3.99

BACKSTREET BOYS – THE ILLUSTRATED STORY
THE UNOFFICIAL BOOK

Sam Hughes

Their millions of adoring fans can't get enough of Kevin, Brian, A.J. Howie and Nick. Their great music and super-cool looks have given them a string of hit singles, and helped them to sell a record-breaking 50m albums around the world. In 2001 the Backstreet Boys got back on the road for another epic world tour, charming their fans and making new friends in every city from Tokyo to Dublin.

Full to the brim with great photos and fascinating facts, this unofficial book tells the full story of how Kevin, Nick, Brian, A.J. and Howie got together and created the phenomenon that is the Backstreet Boys. It's packed with features on the Boys' recent activities, their incredible music and, of course, their love lives!

ISBN 0 7535 0597 5

£3.99

S CLUB 7 – THE UNOFFICIAL BOOK

Mike Roberts

Three boys and four girls with the looks and talent to take on the world, Tina, Hannah, Jo, Bradley, Paul, Jon and Rachel have scaled the heights of the UK charts and have their hearts set on world domination.

The combination of brilliant tunes and their own TV show has made S Club 7 a chart-topping pop sensation, and with hits like the unfeasibly catchy 'Bring It All Back', 'S Club Party' and the instant classic 'Reach', there's no stopping them!

This colourful, photo-filled book introduces all seven members of the club with in-depth profiles and factfiles, and includes info on how they got together, gossip about making their album and the TV series, plus loads of fascinating facts and brilliant photographs. It's everything an S Club 7 fan could want!

ISBN 0 7535 0403 0

£6.99